date label
overleaf.

942.937

HUGHES Trevor

Ruthin

351.308

134
(new)

RUTHIN

CHANGE AND . . . WHAT NEXT?

HUGHES Trevor

Ruthin

This book must be returned by the last date stamped above.
Rhaid dychwelyd y llyfr hwn erbyn y dyddiad diwethaf a stampiwyd uchod.

A charge will be made for any lost, damaged or overdue books.
Codir tâl os bydd llyfr wedi ei golli neu ei niweidio neu heb ei
ddychwelyd mewn pryd.

RUTHIN

Change and . . . what next?

TREVOR HUGHES

GEE & SON LTD.,
DENBIGH

By the same author:

RUTHIN — A TOWN WITH A PAST (1967)

EIGHTY YEARS ON CALL (1971)

Printed and Published by
GEE & SON LTD., DENBIGH, CLWYD, WALES

TO THE MEMORY OF

MY FATHER

DR. J. MEDWYN HUGHES

Foreword

Ruthin: 'Change and . . . . what next?'

'Old men remember . . .' and how fortunate we are that Dr. Trevor Hughes has packed more than eighty years of rich and evocative memories into these pages.

Most of us have neither inclination nor ability to set down our memories, and priceless material is lost to future generations.

Dr. Hughes has gleaned a sheaf of everlasting flowers that will never bloom again. Readers yet unborn will look on them with wonderment and delight.

CHARLES QUANT.

Acknowledgements

No one person can write a book of authority and interest without reference to Standard Works and Authorities; and especially the help of friends. To the latter I offer my heartfelt thanks for their helpful comments and suggestions so generously given. My thanks are due also to the Archivist's Department of the Clwyd County Council, which was not in existence at the time of my first two books (*Ruthin, a Town with a Past* and *80 years on Call*), for their kind help; and also to the Clwyd County Reference Library. I also thank the typists and the Printers for transforming some of my scribblings and jottings into a more or less coherent whole.

I hope the summation of my efforts derived from these various sources will prove interesting and enjoyable.

Introduction

Enormous changes have taken place which have altered the character of this important little country town, especially so during the past fifty years, in which more has been known and discovered than in the whole of time. This has transformed Ruthin and grafted us on to the wider scope of Life and *modus operandi* in Britain. Gone are many of the glories enjoyed in the past.

"'Tis nature's law to change.'

The dominant changes are four in number:

The transfer of our Ancient Castle to private ownership;

Our loss of status and prestige by the town ceasing to rank as a Borough and Assize Town;

The merger of Flintshire and Denbighshire into Clwyd in 1974 with the loss of the County Offices, and our standing as a County Town;

The closure and demolition of the railway between Corwen and Chester.

'Why did we let them go?' Don't let it be said that our apathy was nothing but plethoric composure! Surely our forbears would have put up a much sterner resistance to some, if not all, of these changes. Anyhow *Le jeu est fait* and it's no good crying over milk that is spilt, no expiations will replace that which is lost, but let us hope that we will be favoured some serendipity to compensate us for this loss.

The purport of this work is not by any means derived from personal knowledge and experience alone, but also to a large extent by informative gleanings from eminent authorities, and it must be regarded with all its fallacies as the interpreted ruminations of an old Native of Ruthin, who would prefer to record them now rather than that they should appear as 'mutterings from the grave' at a later date.

Part I

A PLACE ON THE MAP

In the Old Stone Age Britain was not an Island as we now know it, but formed part of the mainland of primeval Europe, and mighty rivers flowed westwards and northwards to a coastline far out into the Atlantic.

It must be assumed that many huge valleys, including our own Vale of Clwyd, are the result of these topographical eruptions, and other phenomenal upheavals and occurrences; bringing with them disaster and loss of life to the, then, inhabitants.

After the Ice Age the New Stone Age dawned and the survivors from these hazardous times which date from millions of years, if not from Infinity, brought a different race of Homo Sapiens to settle in the district. These Neolithic men were the first of three main race elements which have contributed to make up the Welsh. The second race element was the Bronze Age man who arrived on the scene about 1200 BC and he had developed many manual and social skills.

Finally, in the middle of the third century BC came the Brythons from Gaul – the third element in the admixture of peoples, who gave us Welsh people our present character.

So Ruthin (Rhuthun in Welsh) is one of the oldest inhabited areas in Great Britain having withstood all the hazardous upheavals, ravages and other phenomenal disturbances affecting Life and Property.

This little town is situated on the summit of rising ground, 20 miles down the Vale of Clwyd from the Irish Sea.

The Vale commences on the coast at Dyserth, in the North, and extends for about 20 miles to Llandegla in the South, flanked on its East side by the Clwydian Range, in a succession of hills commencing in Moel Fama[1] (which is the predominant feature 1820 ft. high), overlooking the whole area for miles around. After that Moel Fenlli (1676'), Moel Eithenen (1500'), then alongside the Mold road (or Bwlch y Parc) Moel Gyw (1581'), Moel Llanfair (1466'), Moel y Plech (1138') and Moel y Plas (1443'); some of the 'Moels' are capped by *Iron Age Hill Forts; these of course are an interesting and important study in themselves.

On the other (West) flank, the land although elevated, forming the Hiraethog and other small hills does not rise so abruptly, and gradually fades away more or less to the seaboard.

From Rhuddlan in the North, of importance as a port long before Rhyl, running South Eastwards to Llandegla, is bounded on its Eastward side by a range of hills. The strategic importance of the locality was apparent to the early British, and there appears to have been a fortified post in Ruthin long before the

---

[1] *Moel Fama* (This is her correct designation) other versions are Moel Famma (William Davis Jesus Chapel a Handbook for the Vale of Clwyd), 'Moel Famau' (ordnance survey map) and various local handbooks and guides from time to time, 'Moel Fammau').

On 2nd February 1773 there was an extraordinary happening on this mountain an account of which appeared in the Annual Register, a publication from Holywell. 'There was a great fall of snow, the night before last, Moel Famma was heard to utter, as it were deep groans . . at twelve was a loud clap and the vertex of the hill threw up, in the same instant vast bodies of combustible matter, liquid fire rolled among the heaps of ruins. At the close all nature seemed to make a grand effort and rent one side of the mountain which was solid stone, into an hiatus whose breadth seems to be 200 yards. The summit of the hill tumbled into this opening, and the top appears level, which before was almost perpendicular. All is now hushed, but the places where the fire melted the snow, the earth throws out the verdure of May'.

Anyhow, the upheaval and filling in of the hiatus resulted in the formation of a plateau, which has been measured by my grandson, T. H. Bickerton and is E-W 67 yds, N-S 77 yds. roughly 1½-2 acres at this exact site.

This occurrence is discredited by many. In a letter from Mr. A. G. Veysey, County Archivist, Clwyd County Council, has checked the Cilcain Parish Register of the period and found no trace of it mentioned there. But a researcher of the Seismic Research Unit visiting Mr. Veysey's office in July 1981 was of the opinion that the 'eruption' was in fact a bog explotion. I am obliged to Mr. A. G. Veysey for this information.

* The depression caused by the eruption of massive slabs mostly of limestone 500,000 millions of years ago, in the Stone Age, no doubt, resulted in the formation of the Valley and its river bed, down which the river opens into the sea at Rhuddlan.

Norman Castle was commenced in 1277 — this would probably be Castell Coch. It was in existence round about 700 AD having been built of red sandstone, from the surrounding locality, thus bestowing the name of the town from the Welsh 'Rhudd' (red) and 'dinas' (meaning a City). Its name has undergone modifications from time to time in its Welsh spelling. Thus Rhyddyn, Ruthyn, and Rhuthun and others, but finally the last named Rhuthun, must be regarded as the correct Welsh one. Nothing of importance has been documentarily reported before the reign of Edward I, who arrived in Ruthin about 1272. Information and communication would perforce have been passed by word of mouth, and we know how unreliable, with the messenger's exaggeration or imagination, this can sometimes be. Anyhow, this method of communication was still in use during Army manoeuvres up to the time of the first World War. Here is an example, true or false, of a message sent by a commander of an attacking force back to headquarters, 'Send reinforcements, I'm going to advance.', which when it arrived at its destination was, 'Send three and fourpence I'm goinng to a dance!'

But we know that after Edward I's conquest the Lordship of Dyffryn Clwyd was granted to Reginald de Grey, one of the Norman Barons, in 1282, who in turn granted a charter giving Ruthin the status of 'Borough', with its many privileges. The Lordship was passed down to his son John de Grey and so continued under the de Greys for 226 years until they sold the Lordship to King Henry VII in 1508, by which time, in 1470, printing had become introduced by Caxton, along with other forms of communication, and this brought us all in Ruthin closer together, with news of the World, and our own private affairs.

The history of Ruthin from the Norman conquest to the Middle Ages has already been authoritatively and extensively written by various authors and needs no recapitulation, but the substance of these important and thrilling historical events could form the basis of an exciting *Son et Lumière* which will no doubt be staged in more appropriate time than the present.

Primitive people, when there were no maps available, depended on, or bore such knowledge in their minds 'mental maps'. There is enough evidence, however, to show that about the mid-second century of the Christian era, Britain became elaborated and it was here, no doubt, or perhaps much earlier, that Ruthin may have appeared definitely on the map for the first time. Since then the Ordnance Survey maps have been produced by a Government Department, so that ordinary people may be able to read and gain valuable information from them.

There is evidence of animal and human habitation from the excavation of the caves at Bont Newydd, Ffynnon Beuno, Tremeirchion, in the carboniferous limestone (see researches by Dr. Boyce Dawkins, about 1875). In these caves were found flint instruments, bone remains of prehistoric animals (lion, elephant, rhinoceros, etc.), together with a human molar tooth giving evidence of life in Palaeolithic times. Stone Age is of Primitive Man, immediately before Bronze and Iron, but the land formation was much earlier than that.

No wonder, as civilization progressed that there was a drift of human population from the woody, marsh grounds to higher up the slopes, for security against this wild life, and to commence building primitive houses and, later, protective forts.

Many centuries ago the Vale of Clwyd[2] was marsh land as far as Denbigh. The river would have been a wide one, then gradually it would form its present riverbed, which still keeps imperceptibly changing along portions of its tortuous course. Clwyd is the Welsh for hurdle or fence but it would take 'some hurdle' to span the entrance of river into vale so as to act as a barrier against any attempting invader into this territory.

For this in the olden times was the means of ingress in fact the gateway by the river which was navigable for small craft (mainly barges) from the Port of Rhuddlan to Ruthin Castle.

---

[2] *Clwyd.* Many rivers take their names from a single feature on the part of their course and this then is applied to the whole river; the use of fencing in this way can be paralleled in the river names on the Continent. (Prof. Neville Richards). The point of origin of the river Clwyd and its course has been described in a previous book *Ruthin — a Town with a Past* by the present author. The brook (River Arfon) following into the Clwyd at Porth y Dre was covered over in 1875 to make the Wide Street (Mwrog Street).

Denbigh via Rhuddlan to Holland the Continent was the route followed by traders in merchandise, wool, gloves, and bricks for building houses. The tiles forming the three tiers of dormer windows of the Myddelton Arms Hotel in Ruthin and bricks for houses of the estates of Richard Clough (such as Bach y Graig and others) were transported in barges by this means.

Reference to the state of the terrain was made by Iolo Goch (1320-1398) in his manuscripts 'Lleweni Mawr yn llyn o dwr ar Ruthin Yn Tre Harburr' (When Lleweni was submerged by sea and Ruthin a harbour town).

Where then was this 'hurdle' situated? I doubt if anyone really knows for certain, but it was probably near Bodrhyddau-ddwr (The Ford of the two rivers) which is low lying up to a point where the river, after coalescence with the Elwy is tidal.

According to the late Professor Melville Richards 'Clwyd does mean a "hurdle" or "Wattle fencing" and it could have been used for a weir on the river or, even more probably, as a guide to the ford across the river.'

Agriculture

As an industry our way of life was probably introduced by the Romans about 120 BC, who stimulated the tilling of the earth to raise crops to provide food. It was held pride of place in Britain, and still does in this district of Ruthin and other parts, until superseded by the Industrial Revolution. The methods of tilling the land were very different from the ones used today, for then it was done manually using stone-made hooks, sharpened flints, etc. Later, the plough — pulled by man — came into vogue. Then the traction by animals was conceived in which curious combinations of oxen and asses were hitched, harnessed or yoked together to carry out this purpose; this is rarely seen is Europe today. Later, the idea of traction by animals was developed in the Middle Ages, with the intro-duction of the horse collar which revolutionized traction in agriculture. It is remarkable how the horse so willingly accom-modated itself to our needs, undergoing the indignity (in the case even of the cart-horse) of threading its head, with docility, into a 24 lb. leather collar. So that during the passage of time, traction, from the natural means, i.e. pushing, pulling manually, and also floating, has passed to motorized mechanization: and here great strides have been made. With these we have the combine, which mows, reaps and gathers (in some cases dries) the corn in one process — or gathers, shells peas, or beans, or cleans carrots rendering them ready for sale in one operation on the site.

Gone are the happy pictures adorning the walls of our homes depicting nostalgic scenes of 'tea in the hay field', 'shoeing the old grey mare', etc., to the almost extinction of the horse (Clydesdales, Suffolk-Punches, Percherons and the rest). It is to their credit that to this day power machines are rated in terms of so many H.P. Happily though, the call for our old friend the horse for its use in so many capacities is returning.

Tuberculosis eradication, artificial insemination, commonly known in this district as *Tarw Potel* (the Bottle Bull), breeding 'crosses' from different breeds for specific purposes, i.e. the production of milk or beef: and the production of the Santa-Gertruda Cow (which is a cross by the Hereford Bull and the Brahmin Cow) for the dual purpose of milk or traction, were part of the revolution in agriculture.

Then again Foot and Mouth disease — this scourge occurs periodically — but has not now the horrors of formerly — due to the up-to-date methods of dealing with it. Great attention to rotation of crops has been made by most farmers, aerial spraying (seeding and pestical) is carried out by many.

Feeding, by silage, is much more economical than by older methods of harvesting, stooking and stacking crops, in that it retains more of nutrient of the crops and, what is more, the process is independent of the unpredictable weather.

Wonderful advances have been made in the rearing and nurture of farm animals and their diseases; involving the work of scientists in the agriculture, chemical and veterinary professions, and a host of other experts: which are far beyond the scope and knowledge of most of us laymen. Volumes could have been written about these sophistications: some diseases, especially infections, have a habit of recurring from time to time, but

16

through knowledge and experience gained in the past, most of them are effectually dealt with and short-lived, or controlled. Our own district will, of course, share in the benefit of this progress, and retain its pride of place in the farming world for many years to come.

Milling of corn, i.e. by turning and thus crushing one rough surface of stone over another, is of course associated with farming; and the water mill for this purpose has almost entirely disappeared, but some of us older folk can picture the miller emerging from the mill face and clothes covered with flour, imparting on his complexion a 'whiter shade of pale', letting out perhaps a string of five or six little donkeys, unherded on to the roadway, with sacks of flour (one for each animal with the burden divided equally on its back) proceeding unharnessed and unguided in 'follow my leader' style to the appointed farms.

Mills or their buildings are still to be found in Llanrhydd, Pwllglas (Einion Mill), Rhewl (Wern Mill) and other places. Returning to the land, rotation of crops, and silage are fairly recent innovations. The possibilities of extraction from the soil have not by any means been exhausted. These changes have done away with some of the smaller farmsteads of lower acreage on account of their non-viability and expense to conform to modern standards and, hitherto unsuspected for many years properties may be discovered therein. 'Struck Oil', this was the joyful shout in Pennsylvania after discovering that a kind of black glue found in the marshy ground in that district in 1859, turned out, after examination, to be oil. This turned a farming land, unsuspected for 100 years, into a very prosperous oil producing area.

Afforestation

In what was until recently, Denbighshire, forestry was a highly productive and profitable industry comprising the main 17,000 acre Clocaenog Forest, Coed Clwyd Forest (Moel Fama), St. Asaph Forest, Coedygoro, etc. This area has expanded year by year, reaching many thousands more of acreage, to become one of the three largest afforestated areas in the country

17

supplying wood in the form of pit props, material for paper making, to all parts of the country; and it is likely to remain a very important and profitable source of supply for many years in the forseeable future.

Where do we go from here? — Aqua Culture

There has always been, in almost everybody, a fascination for the sea, 'I must go down to the sea again!', and this urge has been answered by many holidaymakers, and others, to go down to the seaside on holiday, for the bathing, paddling or even only to observe the restful rythmical movement of the waves.

The Dolphins

What made the dolphins, those highly intelligent mammals, originally amphibious, forsake the land for the sea? Was it that they preferred to dwell among the sharks of the deep rather than those of the land! And thus bring about curious metamorphosis. Whatever the cause, they have never ceased to exhibit their affinity for human beings. There are several instances of this, i.e. the mythical rescue of *Orion on a Dolphin's back*, (Shakespeare); and other more realistic instances around the coasts of Australia of people being rescued from the sea. Some of us who have visited large aquaria or seen it on television have actually, while bathing in the large pools, ridden on the back of a dolphin. Does this emphasize their desire and affinity to return to their original natural habitat, the sea?

All this does not mean we have any desire in time to follow the example of the dolphins, far from it. We are told that there are many treasures to be found in the deep. From time immemorial fishing has been one of the mainstays of our source of food and is likely to be unless molestation by fishing rights, conflicts between nations for the rights of their 'catches', or other unforeseen hazards which may occur. Already oil is being extracted in vast amounts by numerous 'skiffs' dotted about our seas; and this, being a boost to our economy, is likely to remain for at least the foreseeable future. Then again there is the possibility of the discovery of precious metals, not normally to

18

be found on our shores, and there must be a host of other attractions, not as yet thought of. So far the discovery of metals (sliver and gold) has not been in sufficient quantity for practical usage generally but there may be hopes — who knows. There must be many ship-wrecked vessels of technological and monitory virtuosity lying in the deep with their precious cargoes, some of them containing vast amounts of bullion, to be rescued. One of the latest which comes to mind is the *Mary Rose* (one of Henry VIII's warships, sunk in 1545) which was brought to the surface on 11 October 1982; and there are others.

Communications

Communication between Ruthin and the neighbouring towns, for commercial purposes, was in the fifteenth and sixteenth centuries, almost exclusively by the route of the main Roman roads. Then came the horse-drawn traffic. Within living memory the passenger traffic was provided daily, except Sundays, by a coach, drawn by three horses, between Ruthin and Chester. It would start at 8.00 a.m. from the old Cross Keys in Well Street , and take the old route over the mountain, past the old Iron Gate, between Moel Fama and Moel Fenlli, and Tŷ-Fy-Nain. There would be a strong chain horse in attendance at the Iron Gate, called upon to assist the regular team up the high slope of the mountain, in snowy or boggy weather. This was a frequent occurence, for there were occasions in which some of the passengers themselves had to get out and literally 'put a shoulder to the wheel' to help get the coach moving. After a change of horses in Mold, the whole distance would be transversed in just under two hours, which time was never surpassed by the railway, from its advent in 1860, until its closure. Of course, the railway train with all its comforts and facilities had to pass through Denbigh and around the mountains to get to Chester.

The railway came to Ruthin on 1st March 1862, the first sod being cut by Miss Patricia West on 4th September 1860, and it seems almost unbelievable that by 1965 it had gone, not to be replaced by any such essential and convenient facility. The

19

abandonment of the railway in this part of the country, with communication to all parts of England and Wales, has seen a sad loss as a means of travel both pecuniarily and emotionally to the community, among whom it was regarded as an institution — perhaps not thoroughly appreciated by all, at the time.

As far back as 1912 there was a train which left Euston (The Irish Mail) daily, on weekdays, at 12 mid-day and, after a change at Chester, the passengers for Ruthin arrived at their destination at 5.15 p.m. prompt, and prompt it had to be as there was another train waiting at the station to go on the single line to Denbigh. This time has never been improved upon, as yet; even by road transport — except in the fulness of time by plane or helicopter. Electrification, where it applies, is providing a boon and a success to the travelling public. Would one be too presumptious in suggesting that Beeching, in spite of his brilliant scheme was wrongly 'briefed'; leaving North Wales and some areas not electrified — in fact almost on a shoestring in the case of Ruthin and Denbigh, we are virtually marooned!

Perhaps, the exigencies of the demand for speeding up travel and accommodating 32 ft. long (soon possibly 44 ft.) gargantuan vehicles with their excessive wear and tear of the roads and the inconvenience, caused by their passage through the narrow streets of small towns. Nevertheless, motoring on the whole was pleasurable in spite of the fact that the ladies had to wear large broad-rimmed hats with veils as protection against the dust, which was heavy in dry weather, on the roads.

Before dispensing with the valuable service the horse has rendered let us consider some other purposes for it.

The Fire Brigade

The original 'fire brigade', consisted of a water pump on a rectangular frame, with front and rear wheels on fixed axles, propelled by the pulling and pushing by hand. It was only capable of moving in one direction, and in order to change course or negotiate street corners, or move to the right or the left, the rear portion had to be lifted up off the ground. Anyhow,

20

Fire Brigade (drawn by the author)

it was found to be too heavy for manual propulsion alone, so a pony or a donkey was employed to pull the contraption.

Later came the 'manual', drawn by two horses, with four or five of the Brigade aboard the vehicle.

And, lastly, the steam fire engine (1906), drawn by a pair or four horses, according to the distance to be covered; when a fire broke out in the neighbourhood the 'fire bell' would ring and this was a thrill! Most of the younger people would leave their comfortable firesides and rush to the fire station, to see what was happening. The horses would be there already, also some of the Brigade, and after preparations were complete the driver, who in this case was also their captain (Tegid Owen), would climb into the driving seat. 'All ready?', the driver would draw his whip artistically across the team's shoulders, then with a flourish of his whip, it was 'off to go', full pelt. As boys we would go to the nearest point of vantage to see this intrepid driver take the corner, which he would do with unerring skill, often with two of the engine's wheels off the ground. We do not have an outside fire alarm nowadays, the Brigade is summoned by telephone to the fire station and they move off noiselessly to perform their often complicated duties, but pleasant memories of the past thrilling times still linger on.

The Royal Mail

This was a horse-drawn vehicle driven by the Mail man, and plying between Ruthin and Flint, two journeys were made each day — early morning, i.e. Ruthin-Flint and return and again at night. It was really efficient service, and we were sorry to see it go in 1913, when it was replaced by motor transport between Ruthin and Rhyl.

Later came the transition from horse traction to that of motor (internal combustion engine) transport.

With the improvement in resurfacing, and re-routing excepting some of the main roads, over the roads in rural areas and smaller towns such as ours, required drastic attention, for they were formed by rough flints, strewn on the road base, and embedded in, to some extent, mud. Until 1910 this caused motorists who indulged in this form of transport, then a novelty, to

22

complain that the tyres of their vehicles were expected to provide a suitable surface by passing over the large sharp flints. This called for a substitution from iron to rubber rimmed wheels — at first solid — later pneumatic; and after this correction all road vehicles, carriages, horse traps, bicycles and even wheelbarrows, followed suit, and by and by this extended to the heaviest lorries, large farm vehicles and coaches fitted with this strong, durable and resistant material.[3]

Trade and Commerce in 15th and 16th Centuries

The nobilities, amongst whom were numbered the de Greys, the Myddeltons, the Goodmans, father and son and Sir Richard Clough (the greatest of the merchants of this time) and many others, were not averse to adding to their wealth and so became captains of industry and commerce.

The de Greys were mostly interested in the woollen trade and were Mercers also, as was Sir Richard Clough (who held high office in the State and did most of his trade from Denbigh to the Lowlands, Antwerp and other places). Rhuddlan at this time was a very busy port. Sir Thomas Exmewe, also a Mercer, builder of Exmewe House, became Lord Mayor of London in 1517/18. The Myddelton Arms was built, with the assistance of Flemish Craftsmen, for Sir Richard Clough, 1560/70, by Pendrick Paeschen who came over from Antwerp to design other buildings for him. The names of the Inn have changed from the Myddelton Arms to the White Lion 1874 and again in 1895, to the Castle Hotel and Myddelton Arms. Inside the latter there is evidence of wattle and daub. These buildings faced the Ruthin Old Hall, demolished in 1863, and the Old Myddelton Arms still retains its ancient facade outside.

---

[3] *Rubber.* Latex exuding from rubber trees when the bark is incised resembles milk and indeed it is treated likewise with almost the identical plant for separating, i.e. in the former case cream from water, in the latter rubber from water. *Artificial Rubber: Old book — The Buna Process:* Butyl Diene is polymerized by soda (NA). Butyl diene is a gas but some of its polymers, when treated with Sodium, become very heavy molecules and so a viscid product is obtained. No doubt many modifications in the process of the manufacture of rubber have been made in recent years.

15th Century Cloth Trade

Ruthin was in the forefront of the cloth trade due to the de Grey family. It became the first area in North Wales to belong to the Guild of Weavers, 1447. The complete process of shearing, spinning and fulling (beating and cleaning the wool) was often carried out entirely in the small homes and farmsteads. But, of course, the preliminary processes were not usually carried out in the larger towns in Britain, where large mills were established and skilled work was carried out by machinery to produce the finished article. But, the fulling process was carried out originally at the water mills, and a great deal of running water was required. In Ruthin there was one fulling mill in Llanrhydd, and four others in the neighbouring district doing good business, adding to the trade and commerce not only all over the country, but also in the areas in which the goods were produced.

Printing

The earliest records we have of printers in Ruthin is of Thomas Gee, who was apprenticed to Thomas Jones, Well Street, in 1806. The two men chiefly involved were John Owain and the printer, Isaac Clarke, who lived in Well Street, Ruthin, until his death in 1875. It is not generally known that the song which became the Welsh National Anthem *Hen Wlad fy Nhadau* was printed and published for the first time in Ruthin in August 1860 at the site of what is now known as *Siop Nain*.

Welsh people, the world over, are indebted to the Welsh musician Owain Alan (John Owen) for having the tune, through a competition at the Grand National Eisteddfod in Llangollen in 1858, at which he adjudicated and came across the tune in a collection of unpublished manuscript music. Being so taken by this tune he rearranged and edited it and decided to publish it in *Gems of Welsh Melody* by Isaac Clarke. I am grateful to Mr. Oswald Edwards for this information, which appeared in his article in *Country Quest* July 1973.

Electricity

The source of illumination and heating in the homestead in the old days was by candles, oil lamps or gas. The street lighting was by gas, produced locally in plenty by relays of stokers who, as it were, 'kept the kettle boiling' day and night.

Some of us older inhabitants will remember the lamplighter, whose role it was to light each standard light by a kind of taper, fixed on the end of a pole, at the approach of darkness, and turn it off in the morning when daylight appeared.

It was in 1914 that Ruthin produced its own electricity, through the agency of the Western Electricity Supply Corporation Limited. The source of energy for its production was by a Diesel Engine cooled by the introduction of a military tank engine which served its purpose initially, although it made a frightful din through the night. The first man to look after it at night had instructions to switch it off if he suspected it was not working properly. The story goes that on the first night the noise was so deafening and unnerving, being enclosed in so small a space, that in exasperation he switched off. Of course, the engine was soon replaced by an up to date modern one for the purpose. The electricity supply for the whole country was Nationalised in 1947, and taken over by MANWEB in many parts. One can imagine the discussions in many Councils before the adoption of electricity generally all over the country, and some amusing stories emanated from these meetings. One Chairman (not in Ruthin) voicing his pleasure remarked 'Honour the Light Brigade' with a rejoiner by a fellow councillor not so delighted 'But remember the Charge they made'.

The Telephone

I cannot remember being without a telephone in my home, which was provided by the National Telephone Company (in 1903, I believe) and being a novelty at first the directory would only run into double figures thus:

Ellis Table Water Works	No. 1 Ruthin
E. B. Jones & Co., Grocers	No. 2 Ruthin
Dr. J. M. Hughes (my father)	No. 3 Ruthin

Of course the postal service was in operation for many years previously and one can imagine old Mrs. Jones of Pendrawbyd, saying a loving goodbye to her son, departing for London, 'I will write to you when I get there', the service which would be covered by a One penny stamp, telling her to come. We could continue our fictitious story regarding Mrs. Jones to the time when she would actually set off to carry out her mission. Oh yes! Mr. Evans, a neighbour, would drive her to Ruthin Station in the dog cart, with her luggage packed up in a bandbox, perhaps tied up with *cortyn coch** to fulfil her promised maternal obligation. The LMS train would speed along arriving at Euston in just over five hours which is the time at present (1983) by car/rail, the kind Railway Guards piloting and delivering her safely into the hands of her son who was meeting her.

The Wireless

The Wireless first came to my notice through by brother Wyn, who was deeply 'interested in everything electrical'. He seemed to understand the complicated wiring of the popular excellent model of the Ford car of the early twenties, very unkindly nicknamed the *flying bedstead*. Between times as leader of a local amateur 'Jazz Band', in which he played the Ukelele (which strains were not very much appreciated in the household) and other hobbies — he managed to assemble a 'Crystal Set'. This was, to him, a very interesting and costly hobby to find 'ten bobs' to replace numerous blown valves and leaving all his paraphenalia lying all about the house, so he was bundled out and relegated to the saddle room, a rather dark room lit by an oil lamp, out of the way — but it was marvellous and uncanny to hear the strains of music and voices coming over the air from 5SC, late at night in that room.

'Rome was not built in a day' and this old saying has been experienced in many thousands of communities seeking and striving for progress in the production of the necessities of Life. These desiderata, in the main, apart from the natural fruits of the earth are, heat, light, sound and electricity.

* Cheap binding twine.

26

Water

It is a very long time ago since people had to draw water from the well, or collect it in containers from other sources. It was well before I was born that Ruthin had a piped water supply.

An Act of Parliament in 1860, enabled Ruthin to have its first piped water supply. In 1874 Ruthin Water Works was taken over by a private company of local tradesmen and others, the Secretary of which was John H. Jones of 38 Well Street.

During the last few years all water supplies, except a few private ones which have existed for many years, have been taken over by the Water Board.

It is interesting to note that in the Will of Dean Gabriel Goodman, dated 1600, he reserved 'twenty pounds to be bestowed towards the Conduit in Ruthin, from the Fountain called Galchog, into the midst of the Town of Ruthin . . .' The first water supply to the Town?

Hygiene and Sanitation

With the introduction of piped water into the town, our ideas of sanitation were rapidly carried into effect. Imagine kitchens, wash hand basins, bathrooms, etc., in some homes without this very essential amenity.

The Tŷ Bach

The early 1980's saw the disappearance of this little structure, almost entirely, and very few, if any remain, after measures were taken by the Health Authority to block out this objectionable blot on the environs of some of the smaller homesteads.

It took the form of a small wooden building or shed at the bottom of the garden and housed a dry closet; the excreta of which was periodically covered over with sand or soil. The seat, usually single, was of wood, although there were variations in the number of apertures, from two to even three; although it is difficult to imagine the occasion on which the latter would be used by three persons at the same sitting; nevertheless, the '3 holer' did exist, although very few will be seen nowadays.

27

There are several amusing stories connected with this absolutely essential convenience, one of these is when a contractor was settling up with the owner of the house, after completing the job of installing a WC in his house said 'You won't want the old wooden seat will you?' 'Yes' 'What for?' 'To frame a picture of "Taid" (or some other notability) for mural decoration.' Our standards of hygiene and sanitation, together with other measures will ensure that everywhere people will enjoy better health.

Extractive Industry

There was never any coal mining in this district, the nearest approach to this was quarrying — of which there was one between Ruthin and Rhewl, the limestone from which was fed to a large kiln for processing. An amusing episode occurred some years ago at this site. It was customary for many years to convey the stone from the 'rock face' to the kiln by a truck on rails pulled by a donkey. Eventually the donkey died, and the driver became very upset, and depressed. One of the quarry men asked him why he was so downhearted 'You used to beat and treat him as roughly as any of us others?' 'Maybe', he said, but somebody has got to push the . . . truck and that somebody is me'. The quarry closed down about 30 or 40 years ago.

There was a siding at the kiln by an extension of the main Corwen-Denbigh line LNWR. The line covered a distance of about one mile and ran across the Ruthin-Denbigh Road, at the foot of the kiln; whether it was buried and surfaced by the road or just dug up as 'Any old iron' I do not know, but if it was left there *insitu* it could become a relic of the quarrying activities of the 20th century, as is the evidence of installations of heating and water in Pompei, and unearthed by archaeologists as a 'find'.

Extending from Lôn Parcwr (in Canol y Dre) is a huge area scheduled as an area for industrial development reaching, with only a few spaces apart, as far as the old Lime Kiln. During the past few years large buildings have sprung up with mushroom like rapidity. Here are to be found centres of building material, concrete products, timber yards, coal yards, agricultural machines and other materials, plant contractors of every description — bulldozers, conveyor belt for sale, hire or repair for building or road construction and motor accessories.

But these developments are not only in the heavy industrial field; there is a fast growing occupation in the highly technological production of optical instruments (exclusive of spectacles) for industrial purposes.

Brewing

The first mention of brewing, at the end of the 18th century in Denbighshire was Wrexham; since then many notable breweries sprang in that town. As far as Ruthin is concerned, R. Roberts the Hand (a well known local benefactor) 17/19 Well Street, was the only brewery I know of. It was started at the Corporation Arms, Castle Street, moved to Well Street to become a brewery in 1890. Tiles of *Roberts Home Brewed Ales* have recently been uncovered on the exterior of the Corporation Arms.

Mineral Waters

R. Ellis and Son Limited, established in 1825 in Mwrog Street, employed about fifty local people. The tall chimney, a landmark, was demolished in 1980, the site now being developed with houses.

The Cambrian Waters

Founded about 1854 in Park Road has now been cleared and is being developed for housing. The works, with its Artesian Well, continued as a prosperous concern under this name until taken over, along with a large portion of land for stocking and warehouse purposes, by different firms; the present owners being Cantrell & Cochrane.

It is interesting to note that there is a relic in the form of a 200 gallon tank in the Old Forge in Prior Street.

Crafts and Trades

From Tudor times to the middle of the 20th century many individual trades and crafts sprung up and those that remained until that period were well known to us Ruthin people, and originated as home industries.

Almost imperceptibly over the past half century many of our crafts have more and more become obsolete and in many cases have unostentatiously disappeared entirely. This applies to Ruthin and district in particular, but what is true here must, to a greater or lesser extent, apply to the whole of the rural area of England and Wales, with the exception of some areas where some wheelrights, I believe, practice their craft. There was only one survivor of the wheelrights of Ruthin until 1965. One can remember in the past three separate operators. Things were a great deal more difficult in those days, lathes were not in vogue, neither was acetylene welding. The hub and spokes would be made from wood obtained from elm grown on rocky ground which seemed to impart its hardness into the wood. Such wood was to be found in Cyffylliog. It was a difficult job to make the sockets at twelve equidistant intervals around in the circumference of the hub to receive the spokes, without using precision instruments. The iron rim was forced red-hot onto the wooden circumference of the wheel and metal work was done by hand and often single-handed. One wheelright who came to mind was John Jones, Brynffynnon, Efenechtyd.

The art of the woodcarver is indeed a lost one except in furniture factories. The only one I can remember was Will ('Berri') a wonderful old character with a great sense of humour. He served his apprenticeship in Llanrhydd Mill (mentioned earlier), which was then a carpenter's workshop, served very conveniently by the old water mill. He later was in great demand in many big houses of England and Wales, such as Hyde Park House (now the Yacht Club) and was renowned for his excellent carving. One of Berri's masterpieces is the heavy door of the 1863 Town Hall of Ruthin which he made and, according to his fellow craftsmen was 'beautifully hung'. It retains this property after over 100 years, in that in the full range of movement it

30

will 'stay put', unless pushed or blown by a very strong gust of wind.

I met Berri in 1910 when my father had employed him to cut out and carve an arch of old oak to install over a recess in The Manor House, which was then my home. Having cut the wood to shape and a wooden 'Keystone' in an ornate surround shield he asked me to draw something on the arch for him to carve. Having seen it for many years and become familiar it is still the most extraordinary looking piece of old oak with the two limbs of the arch, with its carved inset in the form of a serpiginous branch commencing at the bottom and ending at the top close to the shield which separated by its fellow branch from one another. From each of the two main branches sprung maple and oak leaves, grapes and roses. It was beautifully carved and it is a pity that there was not a better object for his art — but of course he could not draw. The arch completed, he turned to me with his characteristic grin and he said, talking about the shield in the centre, 'What date shall I put on it?' 'I think we'll leave it for the present' — it is still undated.

The carved arch is still there in its original place in The Manor House, which is at present (1983) undergoing extensive repairs by the latest owner.

Many people have asked him for the recipe of his oak-stain: 'There is no secret' he would say — but his secret has not been divulged, and he has taken it with him to the grave.

It is difficult to understand why *thatching* has become obsolete as it has cheapness to recommend it and entails local labour, and it is certainly more sightly than some of the corrugated iron monstrosities seen on some of the farms nowadays. Some of the objections to the straw-thatched house were that the roof sometimes harboured unwelcomed guests such as rats, sparrows, and, wrost of all bees' and wasps' nests. Certain measures can be taken to protect against the former two by covering with fine mesh wire netting — but that would not exclude the wasps.

The 'Long House' was usually not thatched but it was thought by some that the house part attracted flies and insects from the adjoining stables and shippons. This is erroneous however as the intruders much preferred the warmer comfort of the latter.

David Richard Jones of Sarnedd Gwyn, Derwen, was the only surviving thatcher that I knew and many of the former straw-thatched houses in Ruthin and district bear evidence of his handiwork.

Of all the craftsmen in this age of mechanization and automation the most infrequent to come by is the *bootmaker* — there are many repairers but no bootmaker. Such a man was Robert Hughes, who plied his trade for many years in Fron Heulog, Llanelidan, and he was known for a radius of many miles as a first class craftsman. He did not actually make his wooden lasts, but fashioned them according to the customers' requirements — the hard wearing country styles he cut out from the piece of leather himself.

We must not forget Tom Price, the Tinsmith, who was attached to Beech's, he retired a few years ago after many years' useful and valuable work.

The traditional village blacksmith was primarily a shoeing smith but the craft has undergone such a change during the past forty or fifty years that the real practical shoeing smith has become something of a rarity. I can remember one who took such pride and dignity in his work over sixty years ago. On a fine Sunday, after morning Chapel, he could be seen walking down Well Street in pinstriped trousers, frock coat, white or light coloured waistcoat, silk hat, etc. This was Joseph Williams of Prior Street. Yes, he took a pride in his calling and why not? Another shoeing smith was George Philip Jones, Llanfair Road, who carried out his ploy until a few years ago. He was in great demand in racing and hunting stables for his skilful work — and was invited in July 1966, by a Veterinary Surgeon and Exporter, to go out to Jamaica and instruct some of the young men there in the art of shoeing horses. This he gladly agreed to do and made his depature in November 1966, returning in March 1967 having completed his mission. The art of shoeing horses nowadays is not the only one practised by the black-smiths, who have extended their craft and have become very efficient in the way of making artistic ironwork gates, railings

The Square, Ruthin

The Old Court House, The Square

and the like, and there is not much they do not know about welding in all sorts of ironwork.

Stocks or brakes were hardly ever used in this district for shoeing horses, it was the proud boast of most of them, 'I would like to see the horse I could not shoe without using stocks'.

This was not an extraordinary boast, as most well-trained horses seem to take it as a pleasure in the same way as a woman enjoys a manicure of her hand. The hoof of the horse consists of two parts, the sensitive and insensitive lamina, and woe betide the smith who drives a nail into the former, for it would be just like a dentist touching a unanaesthisied exposed nerve with his drill.

I know of an instance in which a horse, while grazing in a nearby field, having cast a shoe, made its way of its own will and accord to the shoeing smith — like a hurt child running to its mummy — to be reshod.

Tremendous changes have taken place in the mode and production and sale of its products following the pattern of Britain as a whole. The emphasis on the whole is now on wholesale production and many huge estates have been turned over to this purpose — the small mixed farm tenants are not followed by their family, many of whom have to find employment as agents for large agricultural foods and mechanical farm machinery — an industry which is of a very high order. Others become agents, bailiffs or farm managers of very big concerns.

The price of land has risen in many cases by ten times its original value and the stock and appurtenances likewise. I remember when I owned a farm, during the years 1947-1957. A good heifer would cost about £16 and an ewe about £2.10s. Years before this a Christmas goose would cost two shillings and sixpence. So, small mixed farms of cattle, sheep, pigs, poultry, etc., have now become non-viable. It would be almost impossible to commence farming on the scale required, for it would mean hundreds of thousands of pounds. This financial problem sometimes is overcome by the effort of a few wealthy enthusiasts in combination. Of course, farming with its essential flora and fauna must remain for ever, I hope as our mainstay, although its character in many cases changed almost beyond recognition in mode of production, the sale of its products. I remember, as a boy, the Old Fair Days, held monthly, that is over 78 years ago, when anyone, and almost every-one who had any business to transact would come into the town, by horse drawn transport or walking, stay the night in some cases, and lodge in some of the pubs, and there were many with home brewed ale and accommodation and stabling. The animals, comprising sheep, cattle, pigs and horses for sale, would mostly come in on foot early on the fair day, some to the auction and some to be sold on the streets. Yes, I remember well groups of two or three bullocks outside by home in Well Street, which was the appointed street for cattle. Clwyd Street was designated for horses and so on.

With regards to groups of cattle, they would be left in charge of a young farm hand, whose tedious duty it was to see that the animals did not stray from their stand. Occasionally, one or two of them would make a dash for freedom, only to be driven back and returned to where they originally stood, until the owner had returned, after having sought out a prospective buyer. After a few minutes discussion about the price, out would come the buyer's cheque book, also his tongue to moisten the portion to be filled in by his 'copying lead' pencil — after this transaction both would adjourn for a cup of tea or a glass of beer.

Sheep would be driven to the auction or, the more discerning farmer would invite an interested buyer to his farm, where he would sell at a better price. It was known in those days that sheep were worth 20% more on their own pasture. The farmers' wives would come in with wicker baskets laden with eggs packed in chaff, and also one or two basins of butter in the old familiar white with blue ringed china. These ladies would disburse their goods, either to the market or to private houses.

There were numerous stalls for sale of greengrocery and other useful essentials on the market square, mainly on the site of the old Market Hall, which until a few years back was cobbled and delineated by white kerb stones. The whole area has now been covered with tar, mainly to enable ladies with high heels to tread more comfortably!

A very constant feature on fair days was the crockery stall, selling crockery of all sorts, including sets of dinner services, tea services, etc. The sellers were usually very humourous and entertaining in shouting out aloud their wares, such as, in the latter, bedroom requisies would include two chamber pots — 'One for for you and one for the lodger!' These stalls would go well into the night, when the stall would be lit by open oil lamps.

In addition to these would be impromptu sideshows in the form of 'fire eating' and 'fireblow' exhibitions, or 'rope tying' and 'strongman shows'.

With all the changes that have taken place in the past 100 years, our Vale has not lost any of its scenic elegance. The hills of the mountain range still maintain that beautiful mystic purple hue, imparted by the heather. Periodically some of the bracken and gorse had to be kept down by burning, large fires could be seen in the Autumn to carry this into effect, although in these parts the mountain ponies, which were numerous, and many of them destined for work in the pit, to some extent kept the bracken under control by devouring it. It is interesting to note that, while burning was taking place, the ponies would edge up to the fringe of the fire, pick up and chew the hot tasty roots of the bracken, like children rushing to a hot chesnut stall. More recently the clearing of the mountain land has been undertaken by ploughing, sometimes Contour ploughing, then seeding, with noticeable colour effects from purple to green in these cultivated areas.

In spite of the erection of huge barns or sheds as additions to the larger farms, where hundreds of sheep are reared, the countryside has not been spoiled. Lambing sheds were made mainly for the safety of the animals during lambing time, the economy in man (and woman) power, for previously there were rotas of accouchers to be called out in all weathers (usually cold or snowy), day and night. The lambs fell prey to foxes, badgers, large birds and other predators and worrying dogs, if not closely guarded.

There was a case, in this district, a few years ago of a fight between a badger (regarded as a harmless creature by some) and a ewe protecting her newly born lamb. The fight, in which the ewe charged her opponent by successive short butts must have gone on for some time, until discovered by the approaching farmer carrying a hurricane lamp, who ended the unequal conflict by driving the badger away with his stout stick.

Ruthin Castle

Not a great deal has been written about Ruthin Castle and its environment, with its interesting historical features which still persist. To our discredit we, the natives of Ruthin, have not prized them to anything like their full extent. The best account of Ruthin Castle is still Richard Newcome's *An Account of the Castle and Town of Ruthin,* published in 1829 and printed at the Taliesin Press, Ruthin, by Robert Jones.

There are the dungeons, the whipping post, the armoury, the turrets, one with its winding spiral stone stair, the battlements, and of course the moat, a relic of the time when access from the river was the draw-bridge. The latter is not now in existence. The new portion of the Castle was built in 1852-6.

From being an ancestral home of Col. and Mrs. Cornwallis West, it passed into the hands of a clinic in 1923 for the diagnosis and treatment of medical diseases and this persisted until, in my opinion, Ruthin missed the golden opportunity of acquiring this noble edifice, at a very low cost as the County Offices. This procedure would have been benefitting to the County Town as it then was; instead the honours went to Mold with the merger of Denbighshire and Flintshire into the Clwyd County Council at Shire Hall.

The castle then passed into the ownership of the present proprietors who have converted it into a first class modern hotel, much appreciated by visitors and tourists to Ruthin. One of the many interesting features of the place is that Mediaeval Banquets are held there periodically, reminding us all of the glories of that period : and are enjoyed by many from towns far away.

Nantclwyd House

The oldest building in Ruthin, said to date from Saxon times, with its ancient roof, its wonderful timbered structure, filled in part by wattle and daub material, much of which is to be seen

Nantclwyd House, Ruthin

Ceiling at Nantclwyd House

today. Other interesting features are the armorial bearings, the stained glass windows and, above all, the magnificent plaster ceiling in one of the bedrooms, depicting the double Tudor Rose (York and Lancaster), signifying the unification of two houses; and also the pomegranate, the personal badge of Katherine of Aragon who was married to Henry VIII, but does not denote that the latter stayed in this house, in fact there is no record of a reigning monarch *staying* in Ruthin, although King Edward VII (as Prince of Wales) did stay at Ruthin Castle during the Chester Races. The diagram below is self explanatory:

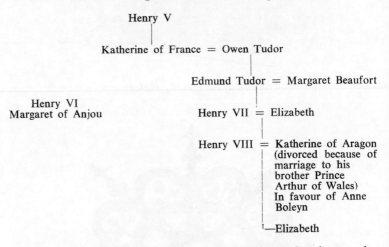

Henry V
|
Katherine of France = Owen Tudor
|
Edmund Tudor = Margaret Beaufort
|
Henry VI
Margaret of Anjou   Henry VII = Elizabeth
|
Henry VIII = Katherine of Aragon
(divorced because of
marriage to his
brother Prince
Arthur of Wales)
In favour of Anne
Boleyn
|—Elizabeth

Nantclwyd House was the home of Gabriel Goodman who was, and remained, Dean of Westminster Abbey, during the whole reign of Elizabeth I. He and his nephew Godfrey, Bishop of Gloucester, will be remembered as great philanthropists and benefactors in Ruthin and district.

The house itself was the Judge's Lodgings for many years until the Assizes were taken over by the Crown Court at Mold in 1972.

After the death of her husband S. Dyer Gough, it has been the residence of Mrs. Jeanne Gough who, very generously, throws it open for raising of charitable funds such as the Cancer Campaign, R.N.L.I. and other worthy causes. The house is the only Grade I Listed Building in Ruthin.

The Manor House

60 or 70 yards down from Castle Street opposite the old street gas standard (see picture) is The Manor House, built during three eras, Elizabethan, 18th and 19th century, of limestone in a wide open space which was a portion of the precincts of Ruthin Castle. A portion of the Old Castle Wall being demolished for the purpose of building the Old House. Later, in the 1780's a cottage, which became No. 10 Record Street was built (eventually becoming the saddle room of the stables for my father's horses, which were necessary to carry out his Medical Practice). With all these developments Record Street came into existence joining Well Street. Of course the old house has been extended and renovated from time to time by its several occupants, notably for dormitory accommodation for the boys of Ruthin School (1800-1865), then by Marcus Louis, a solicitor and very prominent character, who in 1864 was responsible for laying the pavements of the town. When in residence in this house he had the large cellar deepened and during these excavations he discovered a deeper cellar probably in existence 240 or 250 years before the earliest house, on the wall of which was an opening into what was a subterranean system of tunnels said to have existed down the greater part of Well Street and communicating with the Castle. This opening was walled up.

In the cellar there had been a Well, fed by a spring and drained away to a pipe at a lower level. The Well seems to have dried up during the last 25 or 30 years.

Following Mr. Louis came a number of occupants in succession the last being my father in 1900.

It is, by present standards, a massive edifice; containing 8 bedrooms, which of course was required for his growing family of 3 girls and 3 boys. Anyhow we all lived happily, I for 60 years in that spacious building with a small garden in front providing a restful *Oasis* from the busy street outside.

I am grateful to Mr. R. M. Hartford for providing some of the information regarding this old house. The present proprietors have gone to great trouble and expense to replan and renovate much of the interior and it is now a smart and up to date Restaurant, with an attached Bistro at the lower end of the building.

Pentre Coch Manor, Llanfair D.C.

There would appear to be no recorded evidence that Pentre Coch Manor was built by Sir Richard Clough. The studded door with the initials 'RC' probably came from Bach-y-Graig, near Tremeirchion, which was the first house in the Vale of Clwyd to be built of bricks (shipped from Holland). This house *was* built by Sir Richard Clough. The house was demolished by John Salusbury in 1821, having been replaced by the building of Bryn Bella in 1795.

Cordelia Jones, who was the first of four of that very name owned the house until 1821, when it was sold to George Adams (Clerk of the Peace and Ruthin's first Mayor) whose daughter married General Carey.

In my time it was inhabited by the General and handed down to a succession of owners amongst which were Sir Henry Morris Jones, Mr. Whitham, Mr. Herbert Richard Bickerton (ophthalmic surgeon) to its present owner Mr. Peter Howell Williams to whom I am greatly indebted for relating the following interesting episode:

'It is well-known locally that The Manor has a Cavalier ghost. Various owners have believed that it perambulated around the yew tree, the reason why we cut the tree down was because it was poisonous to cattle. When we came to the Manor we noticed the dog each evening barked furiously at the yew tree, but at that time we knew of no ghost. My wife was at home one night by herself and in the middle of the night heard a loud crashing sound which went on for some time. She bravely got up, put on the light, took her torch and went round the house, fearing that perhaps a chimney had fallen in. She noticed nothing. The next morning she found at one end of the bedroom a picture with a cord unbroken, which had previously hung on a nail on the opposite wall. It was a facsimile of the death warrant of King Charles signed by one of her ancestors (amongst others) James Challinor of the ancient family of

Challinors of Denbigh. It was totally impossible for this to drop simply from the wall to the position in which it was found. It was as if the Cavalier ghost was offended by such a picture hanging in the Manor. We were then told about the experiences of past owners and indeed our predecessors sold their four poster bed which had stood in the same bedroom because they thought it was the bed which was haunted rather than the house.

At least two people have sensed a presence but all confirm it is a friendly presence.

In the summer of 1979 we were to hold a Silver Wedding Party and that week dug out the yew tree from the lawn, having fenced in the lawn to provide extra grazing. A three foot long by one foot wide and high piece of granite was carried by three men from the back of the house to the front garden, cemented in and on top was placed a one foot square piece of granite which was also cemented onto the bottom piece.

A great number of cars were in the drives etc., and whilst everyone left late there was no incident in which a car, to my knowledge, hit this mounting block and indeed had they done so the car would have been badly marked because of the strength and weight of the granite. No car could in any event get up a speed which would enable the granite to be moved.

The following morning I came out of the house and noticed that the top smaller piece had been rolled six feet away from its cemented base and the bottom huge piece of granite had been moved some nine inches from its original base. There were no markings on either stone. I could only believe that in some way the ghost had been offended by the removal of the yew tree and had made that gesture in protest.

Ruthin was, of course, a Cavalier area in the Civil War, and there were certainly skirmishes but no evidence has been provided that anything happened in or about the Manor as such, so far we have not been able to identify the owners or occupiers of the Manor at that time.'

Ruthin Almshouses

Ruthin Almshouses in the Parish of Llanrhydd, built in 1840, the gift of Joseph Ablett[4] of Llanbedr, F.R.S., Surgeon, was a very fine stone building which housed 12 residents. Emblazoned on the outside boldly in Welsh on stone was the direction to the effect that this building shall stand as long as water shall flow (*tra rhed y dŵr*).

It was demolished in 1928, leaving no trace of its former existence except a large foundation plaque which is still to be seen on the site, set flat in the ground near the road. It reads as follows :

> *The gift of Mr. and Mrs. Ablett, Llanbedr Hall, for the poor equally of the Parishes of Llanbedr, Llanrhydd, Llanfair MDCCCXL.*

Four stone shields were also taken from the building with the Coat of Arms of Ablett. These are to be seen on the drive leading up to *Awelon* the new Welfare Home.

Ruthin Workhouse

Along with all Poor Law Institutions in this country the Authorities, to their credit, did not allow anyone in need of food or shelter to be turned away from its doors, which is more than can be said of some of the hospitals under various troubles and exigencies, which from time to time arise, in the present time. The Workhouses came under the biting criticism of Charles Dickens, because of the harsh treatment meted out to the residents in some cases.

The Ruthin Workhouse in the Parish of Llanrhydd was built in the year 1837 and provided accommodation for about 110 to 120 people including 20-35 vagrants under the Vagrancy Act. Joseph Ablett, F.R.S., of Llanbedr Hall (a well known benefactor of several institutions in the Country) was its first Chairman, and he held this position for many years.

---

[4] *Joseph Ablett* (1773-1848) who lived in Llanbedr Hall, built old almshouses in Ruthin as a gift for the poor of the parishes of Llanbedr, Llanrhydd (of which Ruthin was a part). He was succeeded by a remote relative, John Jesse, a surgeon, who was also a benefactor. He built the present Church at Llanbedr and also gave the East Window of St. Peter's Church at Ruthin.

It is unfortunate that the institution of the workhouse in this country came under the harsh criticism of Dickens. Those of us who have read Oliver Twist cannot have had anything but a poor impression of the workhouse with all its defects. It was a new concept, and necessarily there were imperfections, which the Boards of Guardians strove to overcome : and many of them successfully. But all workhouses, in spite of initial lack of experience in administration did not follow the pattern of cruelty, rough handling, and lack of understanding, as in the case of John Rowlands, who as a boy absconded and became, as Henry Morton Stanley, the great explorer, journalist and discoverer of the Nile. Far from it, many of the houses became a refuge from the hard conditions of this life; and came under the care of the Master. This person was not one depicted by many as a gruff and heartless individual; on the contrary my experience as a Poor Law Medical Officer, over a period of many years, and I have known quite a few of them, to be reasonable, kindly and sympathetic men; strict, if you like, and having a regard for discipline. This latter quality was essential in dealing with all sorts and conditions of men, which included rough and ready vagabonds, nomads, and various species of itinerant vagrants — none of which could be turned away from admission to the Institution. This is more than can be said for the discrimination for hospital admission during periods of industrial unrest. But there was a great deal of happiness and contentment in many of the institutions; there were so many cases of admittance of lowly persons requiring help and security to a great extent, to their local conditions of environment. Here is a true story of a nearby workhouse. In this institution Sunday services were conducted regularly, there being a rota of ministers—each service vix. Anglican Church, Calvinistic Methodist, Presbyterian and Baptist; which were well attended and enjoyed by most of the residents, especially a very devout old lady, whom we will call Mary Jane. Of course, they all had their favourites. Mary Jane, who could not contain her feelings and emotions would get the better of her, would stand up in the middle of the sermon, shouting *Haleliwia! Diolch Iddo* (thanks be to God) and so on. The others complained to the Master about these interruptions;

and he called the lady to his office. He told her of their complaints, and informed her that in future she would not be allowed to attend the service on account of her behaviour. At this, the old lady, was very upset, wept copiously and pleaded that this should not be so. Anyhow, the Master relented and said 'Well, if you promise to behave during the next three Sundays, I'll allow you to. What is more I'll give you a pair of elastic-sided shoes' (*esgidiau-lastig* — a much prized possession in those days). Came the first Sunday, the Church of England parson preaching, and he was very good, but with a great effort she managed to restrain herself. Next Sunday, the Calvinistic Methodist preached — he was also good — but with difficulty she again managed to restrain from interrupting. So far so good. Then, on the third Sunday, came the Baptist Minister, her special favourite, and she was moved so thoroughly by his sermon that in the middle of it, in her fervour, she forgot her promise to the Master, stood up and shouted, *I'r cythraul efo'r hen meistr a'i esgidiau lastig; Iesu Grist i ni.* (To hell with the old master and his elastic-sided shoes, Jesus Christ for us'!).

The Merllyn, Llanfair D.C.

This old building now used as a farm outbuilding was the birthplace of Dr. Godfrey Goodman (born 28/2/1582) son of Edward Goodman and nephew of Gabriel Goodman. It was to the latter two that we owe the benefaction of the Ruthin Hospital Charities. Godfrey Goodman became Bishop of Gloucester in the reign of Charles I, in the 1600's. He died on January 19th, 1655 in the Catholic Faith, having turned in his latter years to become a professed Romanist, as appears in his Will.

Jesus Chapel (or Capel y Gloch)

One must recall the history of this curious building founded in 1619, by Rice Williams, Verger of Westminster Abbey, London. This man, a native of these parts, was the only survivor of the street in which he lived in London in the time of the Plague of 1665 (which was ended by the Great Fire of London in 1666). He was appointed an executor of Gabriel Goodman's

Will, after having served him as a verger at Westminster Abbey and 'bell-ringer', not ringing the church bells, but ringing a hand bell before the commencement of each service.

On returning to his native country he founded Jesus Chapel (or Capel y Gloch) in the Parish of Llanfair D.C. as a chapel of ease. Fortnightly Anglican Church services are still held at this chapel, on which occasion the bell is rung. It is also rung on Christmas Day and on other special occasions.

A full account of this Chapel of Ease is to be found in William Davis's (Jesus Chapel) handbook 1856 for the Vale of Clwyd.

SOME OLD BUILDINGS

‡St. Peter's Church

Dedicated to St. Peter in 1310 by John, son of Reginald de Grey. It was endowed for a Prior or Warden and few regular priests to perform Mass at Llanrhydd, the Castle Chapel and Parochial Church. The present incumbent still retains the title of Warden.

The Restoration of the Roof took place in 1865; the New Organ was installed in 1902. The following extract is from the Vestry Minutes (St. Peter's Church) re-building of spire in 1859:

> Be it recorded that the first stone of the new spire was laid on the 13th day of July, 1858, by the Rev. B. O. Jones, M.A., Warden*, in the presence of James Maurice, Esq., Mayor, and Churchwardens and a large concourse of the parishioners.

Llanrhydd Church

Llanrhydd Church (St. Meugan's) dates from as early as 7th Century. It was founded by St. Meugan, the patron saint of travellers to whom it was dedicated, and is the mother Church of Ruthin.

‡ For a full history of the Church and adjacent buildings see *Official Guide to St. Peter's Church* published by the Parochial Church Council in 1976.
* Immortalized by Thomas Hughes in *Tom Brown's Schooldays* in the character of Slogger Williams.

Ruthin Gaol

Ruthin Gaol was built in 1775 and many of the residents will remember that the last execution took place in this gaol in 1903 (previous to this the last one was in 1824) and the escapades of that likeable old vagabond *Coch Bach,* who met his death after his escape from the gaol in October 1913.

The prison was closed, and ceased to function in 1916 and the premises are now occupied by the Library and Archivist's Department of the Clwyd County Council.

County Court

This was built in 1785 and is reminiscent of the Assizes, with their grandeur and their ceremony dating from the Middle Ages. These were held for the Law Sittings every quarter, i.e. :

Hilary   — January 11th to March 25th
Easter Term — April 7th to May 15th
Trinity   — May 26th to July 31st
Michaelmas — October 1st to December 21st

The Hall was used for meetings of the Denbighshire County Council and is still used as the Magistrate's Court.

St. Peter's Square

If we take a look at the pictures (Fig. 1) of the market square at the end of the last century we shall find that the whole area was cobbled, with an extention down as far as the Castle gates, and from Castle Street down the whole length of Record Street. I well remember this latter portion being cobbled. It will be noticed that the Old Market Hall, which was built in 1663 from the stones of the North Chancel of St. Peter's, which fell into ruin during the Civil Wars, is not included, neither is the Clock Tower, which was built in 1883 and commemorates Joseph Peers, who was Clerk of the Peace for some fifty years.

On the left of the picture was Exmewe House, next to which was a balcony of the Beehive, which served as a point of vantage and safety during the bull baiting episodes, the area being known as the Shambles. In Exmewe House were the business premises of R. Ellis & Son, Mineral Water Manufacturers in 1825. I knew Exmewe House, in the beginning of the 20th century as being the residence and shop of Theodore Rouw, the Chemist and Italian warehouseman. This latter building was demolished and replaced by Barclays Bank in the 1920s.

At the far end of the square (white building), is the Bank of the Eidion Du (Black Cattle), prominent in the time of the Drovers (there was about this spot in olden times a Priory). Much later it became a public house (the Queen) and, later still, a shop known as Hughes the Stores. The shop was gutted by fire in the night time of 1908. When I and a friend went to inspect the damage on the following morning, samples of biscuits from the tins were nice and warm!

The Myddelton Arms which has offered hospitality and accommodation to travellers since the 16th century was amalgamated with the White Lion, to become the Castle Hotel. The Castle Hotel still remains with the adjoined Myddelton Bar.

Next to the Castle Hotel was a draper's shop, R. Harris & Jones; which was demolished in the early twenties, and replaced by the Midland Bank. Across the road, Market Street, which was made the road to the Railway Station, by demolishing the old Bull Hotel, is a large shop, formerly held by R. Beech & Son, Ironmongers, but now recently taken over by the Western Carpet Company.

Completing the Square was the Old Lordship Courthouse and Prison which dates from 1401. Under the eaves of the west frontage, a portion of the gibbet can be seen. Many transformations have been made in the interior, during the present century from a grocers and ironmongers stores, to an ironmonger stores to a boot shop attached and now, with massive restoration in early 1925 to the National Provincial Bank, now called the National Westminster Bank.

Well Street

Leaving St. Peter's Square we now come to Well Street which figured prominently in the times of Earl de Grey, and today still runs continuously with Clwyd Street, the main street running through the town. It is said that the only houses which escaped the ravages of Owain Glyndŵr was No. 2 Well Street, and the other of course being Nantclwyd House.

Going back to my childhood, I remember No. 2 as being the Post Office.

There was a time when there appears to have been an arbitrary line of demarcation separating the Welsh from the English: this would roughly be along the space occupied by Well Street which in Welsh is *Stryt y Ffynnon* and, to my mind, is a misnomer and should be Welsh Street and the street will, in years to come, probably be restored to its pristine designation. But this distinction is past history and forgotten hundreds of years ago when Ruthin remained subdued by the English invader. All the natural subversiveness and restlessness that existed from the de Grey times, and all the emnity between English and Welsh existed until early in the 15th century is forgotten.

In ancient deeds from the 16th century until the middle of the 17th century, Well Street, was known as *Talysarne*. In the Church Mize Accounts for the 18th century, Well Street is always referred to as *Welsh Street*.

Lower down the street was the *Hand** at the back of which was the famous 'Hand Brewery' (now defunct) owned by R. Roberts. Still lower down is the Wynnstay Arms (originally the *Cross Foxes,* the spacious garden in front of the hotel was dispensed with to make a road — Wynnstay Road — better known to some of us today as New Road. This road joins Well Street with Market Street.

Next to the *Wynnstay,* with a small lane known as 'Dog

---

* This is the sign adopted from the gloved red hand, by some hotels and public houses in Ruthin, Chirk and other places. Sir Thomas Myddelton purchased Chirk Castle in 1595, and the Myddelton Coat of Arms, with the Red Hand above the Crest (mystery surrounds the derivation of the hand and there is no conclusive explanation as to its origin) has been in evidence on the famous gates of the Castle for several generations. The Myddeltons, who followed the Thelwalls of Ruthin Castle, also owned the Myddelton Arms (finally named the Castle Hotel with the original Myddelton portion, now used as a bar), and provided hospitality and accommodation for many travellers since the 14th century. The Hand, in Ruthin, definitely derived its name from the Myddelton Arms.

The Manor House, Ruthin

Well Street, Ruthin

Lane' intervening, is 'Plas Coch' now taken over by the Conservative Club. The Thelwalls moved from their residence in Plas-y-Ward, Rhewl to Bathafarn Hall, thence to Plas Coch. Mercifully, with the addition of Welsh nomenclature the lane has not been changed. It has nothing to do with dogs on lawful or unlawful occasions, but refers to the ancient district of Dogfeiling.

Ruthin School (Schola Ruthinensis)

Refounded by Gabriel Goodman in 1574, the old school was built to the north of St. Peter's Church, the main portion being the spacious Elinor Memorial Buildings until 1892. The present school was built in 1892 and the pupils moved to the new site on Mold Road in August 1893. In Prior Street, across the road from the Old School, was a Pub popularly known as the *Slip in and slap out,* which was frequented by some of the pupils in the old days who 'Slipped in' and after being chased were 'Slapped out" by the masters!

The history of Ruthin School, with all its proceedings and traditions is embodied in a book, still extent, entitled *Ruthin School (The First Seven Centuries),* by Keith M. Thompson.

My first association with Ruthin School was when my father (Dr. J. Medwyn Hughes) became a Governor and School Doctor, and remained a ssuch until his death in 1924. I was sent, as a pupil, to Ruthin School in 1905 and was joined by my two brothers, younger than myself, who remained for various periods until 1916. I left school in 1912 and early in 1915 joined the forces. In 1924, immediately after the death of my father, I was appointed School Doctor by the Headmaster, E. W. Lovegrove, M.A., and remained in that capacity until 1936.

I was honoured on three or four occasions, being the oldest Ruthinian available, by being asked to perform the mournful duty of reading the Roll of Honour of those who fell in the First World War, many with whom I was privileged to serve.

On one occasion I felt moved to quote a portion of a poem written by a young officer, an Old Ruthinian, early in 1915, and quoted in my book *Ruthin, a Town with a Past.*

49

It reads as follows:

> I am lying under cover in a damp and dirty trench,
> Writing High Explosen Stories to a much believing wench,
> Of the deeds of might and valour I've continually done,
> How I led a charge at midnight, How I grappled with a hun.
> But it's all imagination and my conscience gives a wrench,
> As I'r 'lieing' under cover in a damp and dirty trench.
>
> I am lying under cover in a damp and dirty trench,
> For the Battle is commencing, we're defending with the French
> It's all a deafening thunder and the shrapnel's bursting low,
> For the Germans in their myriads are attacking us and so,
> We are waiting to receive them, our revengeful thirst to quench,
> For I'm 'lieing' under cover in a damp and dirty trench.
>
> Yes, I'm lieing under cover in a damp and dirty trench,
> Every stir becomes a torture every movement now a wrench,
> For my life is slowly ebbing, as with blood the ground I drench,
> For I'm 'lieing' under cover in a damp and dirty trench.

This might well have been his epitaph, for he was killed a few days later whilst attempting to bring in a wounded man. He was 2nd Lieut. J. A. Elias Hughes.

The School is flourishing in every way since it was refounded by Gabriel Goodman in 1574. It will be remembered that he remained Dean of Westminster during the whole reign of Elizabeth I and it was most appropriate that, and indeed fortunate, the School should be honoured by the presence of Her Majesty Queen Elizabeth II, on its Seven Hundreth Anniversary on 16th March 1984. This was a tremendous success and a very memorable occasion.

Floreat Schola Ruthinensis

and God Save the Queen.

Taylor's Castle

This structure, on the mountainside close to the Clwyd Gate Cafe, has only recently been built. Far from being a folly, which was regarded in the past as an indulgence, it is of special importance and interest. It was designed by John Tayor (whose parents lived for some years in the Llanbedr area) of Chapman Partners, London. At first the application for planning permission was refused by the Local Authority but later, being supported by Sir Clough Williams Ellis and Lord Esher, permission was granted by the Welsh Office.

This building, a four storey castellated tower, consists of three bedrooms, two bathrooms, a kitchen and an integral garage. Unlike all previous follies it has insulated walls, double glazing and central heating and it is being lived in. It was built by local labour, and material from the neighbourhood.

In years to come, it will be an object of intense interest, being a relic of 20th century building.

Part II

T'is Nature's Law to Change
Constancy alone is strange

JOHN WILMOT (Earl of Rochester)

What a dull place this world would be were it not for change which is the essence and yardstick in the measurement of time, and the rapidity at which it has come upon makes many of us feel that the future has come too soon, and we are not yet fully prepared for it. Anyhow, whether we like it or not, it has come upon us and we must not look back, although at times the memory of some of the pleasantries and extravagancies of by gone days come tippling along gaily through our nostalgic minds. No doubt similar assessments of the present will be considered 'halcyon', by future generations. In the present century, especially during the last fifty years, the changes have been world-wide, and this applies to the whole country, especially since we have suffered the loss of an Empire, and have not yet adapted ourselves fully to a more limited role.

Far more has been known scientifically, technologically and in other ways during the past fifty years, than has been acquired since the beginning of time: and this is presented to the upper form schoolboy 'on a plate'. It is from here that advantage of this 'know how' must be taken to solve our present pressing intricate problems in the development and furtherance of all our natural and inherited gifts, which are many.

Life must go on, whether following and conforming to ever increasing sophisticated technological advances. Of course, this does not apply to our little town alone, but to everyone, in spite of the passing or 'phasing out' of some of our time honoured and ancient institutions and customs, which many of us deplore.

In the past production depended on increasing the number of men on the job : when such magnificent erections as the Telford Bridge over the Menai Straits, or the Aqueduct at Froncysyllte for example were built, when the work, for the most part was done manually — there were no conveyer belts, hydraulic lifts, bulldozers, and other necessary accessories available. The same applies everywhere, in the mines, factory, motor works where there is no shortage of manpower; computerization has superseded much of the time consuming and tedious work formerly done by hand. The enterprise and vigour in presenting such schemes and carrying them out is to be commended, and no doubt will be repeated time and again.

So Ruthin cannot now be regarded as a close entity of a small County Market Town, dependent mainly on agriculture for its way of life, favoured for many years with the dignity and status of Borough, and the pre-eminence of being the County Town of Denbighshire — the latter through the hard work and bargaining of our immediate ancestors, in the struggle in which 'no holds were barred'. Alas these days are gone, and Ruthin has become part of a whole which we must accept, as is the present trend and pattern generally and important local decisions do not rest with influential personalities but are vested in Committees with, often, little thought of their ecology and with no one really left to 'carry the can' of responsibility for their efforts, good or bad.

The Population

In spite of what might be regarded as 'fair wear and tear', that is in deaths, limitaton of families, birth control, movement of families to the district from some of the larger towns and other ecological factors (who would blame those migrating from the town to the country?). Certainly not the indigenous inhabitants — 'live and let live', they are welcome and will be expected to play their part in the resurgence of Ruthin, the population has remained constant at about 4,300 during the past fifty years.

Time was, when walking down the main street one would know, or at least recognise, almost everyone; that is not so today.

53

The balance has changed considerably as between us, the indigenous and migrated inhabitants — due to redeployment. This is most marked in agriculture, on which we were for many years dependent, by the sway, for economic reasons, into industrialism. In many cases tenants of large estates who regarded their standing as a permanency, had to leave their farms and small holdings, because of their non-viability under present conditions (howbeit the transition was made as gently as possible). This means that their sons and daughters were not to succeed them, and sought employment elsewhere as agents in farm products or machinery or other jobs associated with farming the pig or two (the 'gentleman who paid the rent'), and the few poultry concerns had to be disposed of; this was a very saddening event for many.

Again, the transfer of the County Offices, employing 200-300 people, to the Shire Hall, Mold, caused great disruption amongst employees who had been born and bred in Ruthin — some however found the change acceptable, many didn't.

The population has not changed numerically during the past ten years as is shown below. Here are the figures:

In 1961, the population was 3,502. There was an increase from that time until 1971 of 806, bringing the total to 4,308. From 1971 until 1981 the population has remained at practically the same level, i.e. an increase of 92, to 4,400.

Before the year 1925, there was no question of limitation of the family, parents having six or seven children was quite common between 1895 and 1922, or even as many as twenty children, as was the case of John and Elizabeth Edwards, who then lived in Rhos Street. (John was, for many years, Bandmaster of Ruthin Town Band). But this productivity for having children does not exist, for various reasons, nowadays.

Housing

236 Council Houses were built by the Local Authority, and more than that number since the last War.

Employment

There is no need to dilate on unemployment. This sad state of affairs has arisen from many causes — many sources are to be held responsible, such as technology (which, no doubt, will enable us in time to discover or rediscover many of the indigenous and abundant natural resources), the closure and demolition of various long established firms, such as Ellis's, *Cambrian,* and the transfer of the County Offices to the Shire Hall, Mold, brought about an unsettling effect. The result is that many of the Ruthin population paying rates and taxes have to travel daily to find their employment in other places.

To combat some of these changes great emphasis is laid on the project of Tourism, for which Ruthin is ideally situated, where it not for the sparse 'parking facilities'. Sites for parking grounds, although offered, have sometimes been declined for various reasons.

Business and Commerce

The future has come too soon for many of us and we are unprepared for it. We have not accommodated ourselves to the soaring rise in price of almost everything, including the cost of living and household and other materials. From many small beginnings, Ruthin has kept pace with the rest of the country in modernizing its idea of shops, whether it be in food, apparel or household goods, etc. 'You name it, we have it'. Recently the supermarkets have made their impression on the trade of provisions, etc. but not to the extinction of the shopkeeper, who in some cases and for some commodities is more convenient for a source of supply. No! the 'shop around the corner' must remain in its pristine importance to supply our store of provender for many of the culinary necessities.

Country doctors were not the only ones to be disturbed during mealtimes as one grocer told me many years ago. 'My business closes on Sundays and for a dinner hour on weekdays, and it is quite a common thing for a child being sent by its mother during closing hours for a 'pennoth of vinegar'. Well, 'the customer is always right'. Ruthin has become a very up to date shopping centre especially in ladies' dresses and apparel and bookshops, etc., and people from the Wirral, Liverpool, Chester and other neighbouring towns, and the ladies especially, enjoy their beautiful excursion down the Vale, into Ruthin to shop. This is, of course, in part a feature popularising the tourist trade.

Craft Centre

A recently completed novelty has been created in Ruthin and is believed to be the first of its kind in North Wales. It comprises many of the Arts and Crafts, where these may be viewed, demonstrated and/or purchased. It already has become, and likely to be a further attraction, for Tourism, for the environs, the Border Counties and, no doubt, people from abroad.

With all the enormous progress which has been made, Ruthin cannot now be considered an entity as a Country Market Town, a Borough and an Assize Town as formerly.

In recent years, as in other places, a great deal of attention — perhaps too much — has been paid to its commercial prowess with not so much emphasis on Nature with its unbounded source of supply of raw material with its high potential which has not yet been fully exploited, and its possibilities for happiness and enjoyment of life. We have almost imperseptically slipped into an electronically controlled environment.

In this fantasia many think they have come up with a correct version, but so far they are far from evolving a solution and we have been introduced into an electronically controlled environment, whether we like it or not. We must look to technology to redress the imbalance, which must ensue in time, even if slowly.

To attempt to recapitulate and cover even a small portion of the recent discoveries, inventions and innovations which have come into being in recent years, would be a Herculean task, not to be undertaken by the lay man (or woman).

Many of us have tried to listen intelligently, or listen to learned discourses on the Media and, although we think we have got hold of the general idea, when it comes to understanding the practicalities of any of them we come to an abrupt halt.

Nevertheless it has already come into general usage in medicine (heart pacemaker, X-rays with allied aid of scanners), in commerce (the ready reckoners, video tapes) and in the home (Micro-Wave ovens and time pieces etc.). And many dear old ladies, gloating of their enjoyment of the 'good old times' are unsuspectingly wearing electronically controlled watches. Wonders never cease — we have very recently been introduced to the fibre optic fence — used for security purposes.

Perhaps the most outstanding of these highly sophisticated time and life saving discoveries and inventions, is the micro-computer, which appears to be able to do most things that the human brain can do, but not to think; that is, it has no motivation or conation — it can merely reproduce, almost miraculously, what is put into it. It has only been in existence for a short while, not long enough to have its potentialities exploited. Nevertheless, we shall be intrigued to listen to and observe a game of chess played by two computers, or a matrimonial argument between m and f of the same. Finally, let us hope that with the further development of this wonderful adjuct and with the help of the wise counsel of human beings, the futility of a world of war, in which no side can prove victorious, may be averted for good and all, where all these desirata prevails.

In the meantime, with the addition of more recent novelties in the form of telescopes, 'bugging apparatus' etc., we must proceed with caution and not allow these to penetrate into our 'private lives' too deeply, as I am sure most of us have an abhorrence to Peeping Toms and Eavesdroppers.

As the horse collar revolutionized the method of tilling the land, and traction in all its known forms, so three or four hundred years ago did the advent of the wheel. One remembers in one's childhood pictures in books showing the introduction of the wheel barrow which, in some parts of the then uncivilized world, was not fully understood, the labourers carrying the loaded barrow on their heads — this continued for a very short time — until its proper use was explained. Later, the wonderful invention of the wheel came to be used for all purposes of locomotion and traction on the land — imagine a plough without wheels! Then came the cart and the carriage, and the tram —

horse drawn at first. Later came the bicycle (one remembers the old penny farthing type), and the tricycle.

There has always been an urge to get about with all speed as quickly as possible. The first means, although not on wheels, were the ice-skaters, many years ago. These were followed by roller skates only suitable for employment on smooth surfaces, then the skater boards which, because of their instability, were the cause of serious accidents to life and limb, however, they enjoyed their popularity for some time. Then came the glider and also the wind surface yacht, all leading to the possibility of man being able to fly.

It is surprising how the agility and precision of those Olympic Athletes and other Gymnastics can assume all seemingly impossible postures and movements unthinkable a few years ago, propelling themselves off the ground without the aid of spring boards and performing backwards and forward somersaults. Surely this wonderful adaptability will lead, with the aid of some mechanical device, to fly — is this possible or too fantastic to contemplate for many years to come? If not, then the mythical Icarus story will be blown sky high! Of course the idea of feathered wings would not be drawn into consideration, Technology must lead the way. Continuing this fictitious theme, only the very fittest and highly trained athletes would be counted within this coterie (arthritics and anybody with any mental or bodily ailment would be counted out!). Imagine being swooped down on from the sky by one of the more hawklike characters of our friends or rivals demanding the payment of that ten quid which you owed him after the races two months ago or 'hush money' if these transactions and agreements are still extant!

Of course, this state of affairs cannot be countenanced as inconceivable at the present time, and probably not in our time, and for perhaps hundreds of years after.

Since the middle of this century mechanical traction, in all its forms, has taken pride of place and, in this respect, has displaced the horse — though not entirely.

We are loath to say goodbye to our faithful friend for his invaluable service to us in agriculture and commerce and he is, happily, still retained in many spheres, for instance in agricuture where the heavy machines have rendered the arable land to very hard consistency and less suitable for the growth of crops and for other means of transport. His courage, power and gentleness has always been appreciated, especially in sport and other riding exercises. Some of us have come unceremoniously out of the saddle 'via the front door' only to be patiently waited for, lying on the ground (never being trampled on) to be remounted. Lastly we must commend his road sense — a very much called for quality in these days.

Going back seventy or eighty years we read about transport by floating (the least expensive form) in Canada and picture huge logs floating down the river in the Rockies or, in Burma, logs being collected by elephants skillfully and uncannily, with their trunks, and depositing them in the required situation to be thrust into the rivers to be carried down to the seaboard, where they are transferred to ships to be shipped to various destinations.

The first motor car I saw in private use was very early in 1900 in the form of a Mercedes (I think it was). It was coloured (painted) dark green, had solid rubber tyres and the steering was controlled by a handle (similar to those used on steam traction engines and other heavy vehicles used in those days). If it was the one specified below it belonged to Elliott S. Currey of Fachlwyd Hall, Ruthin (Cyffylliog). Registration No. CA 229, 12th March 1907, 15 H.P. Coventry Humber Type, Rovide Belges Body, side entrance, Cape Cart hood. It was driven by Owen Jones, their Chauffeur and the steering arrangements were quite adequate considering the speed limit then, which was, I think, 20 m.p.h.

No! there was no necessity for being preceded by a man waving a flag, although I have seen this meausre employed on the railway along the Liverpool docks.

But let us get back to earth, far from being a pleasurable pastime only, motoring is not leisure as it was 30 or 40 years ago. Although, even in those days the tempo was slow! Ladies with broad rimmed hats and veils, to counteract the dust picked up by the wind and other nuisances (when many of the roads had not a metalled surface).

Nowadays there are other hazards and inconveniences such as

the Insurance of your vehicle, compulsory wearing of a seat belt which the authorities claim is necessary (I have known persons who have been projected out through the windscreen) and 'parking' regulations, which have become necessary owing to the increased volume of motor traffic on the roads. Another added difficulty is driving at night in rainy weather, the illuminated globules of rain falling in front of the driver present an added risk to safety.

Parking difficulties exist in many places, which causes a loss of time and one's patience. Until a short time ago the difficulty was overcome by one driver driving in to town for shopping by horse and trap, 'Ah, but what about parking.' No problem! The yellow lines are designed for motor traffic and if the horse is left facing away from home he will not stray so long as he does not obstruct the traffic. But if you pulled up facing home, what then? He pulled out a chain dog lead, with a 'T' end piece, which he would clip on to the horse's bit and the 'T' dropped into the nearest sewer grid. This ruse lasted for a short while and, no doubt, the Traffic Control Authorities tumbled to it. Anyhow it was an idea.

With the increase in volume of motor traffic which includes gargantuan vehicles in the form of livestock carriers, heavy agricultural and road making carriers and other vehicles besides possibly causing damage to architectural excrescences, such as the upstairs window frames etc., let us hope that in our time no regulation will be introduced for the limitation of the use of the motoring public, in the form of our having to 'book' the road officially!

We are living in wonderful times! This banality, so glibly repeated by many, still rings true, and wears well. We are proud and should be thankful for it. Where shall we begin to recount so many discoveries, let alone place them in correct chronological order, of the past century?

The first that comes to my mind is the 'Magic Lantern' closely followed by the cinematograph, then the 'talkies' (later improved upon by being coloured and even shown in three dimensional pictures), thank goodness we have not yet reached the 'smellies' stage!

Then there was the wonderful X-ray (1895) the Roentgen Ray with which is associated the name of Professor Wilhelm Conrad Roentgen and, later, came the *Wireless* and it was really uncanny to hear voices and music transmitted from many miles away, received in our own homes on a wireless set. This was followed by television, first in black and white, later in colour. We are now able to see and hear 'live' events from all over the world in our homes.

Nuclear Energy

Nuclear Energy with all its terrific potential for good or evil is with us and it is up to mankind to see that it is directed through the proper channels. We owe it to Ernest Rutherford (1871-1937), for the identification of the Atom. It is described as a loose structure of electrons surrounding a heavy core, the other things when released, its terrific powers of destruction and devastation. This was exploited in highly sophisticated research by our scientists forming the atom bomb. This was unleashed by direction of President Truman, two atom bombs being dropped, whatever good or otherwise (and there are many such as the in 1944, one on Hiroshema, the other on Nakasaki with terribly devastating tolls on human life and property over a vast area; the effect of which was manifested, and still is being, and likely to. Whether the decision to drop the bomb was correct from the humanitarian point of view is still being debated. As far as Britain and America, the main opposing great powers concerned, it put an end to the fighting in the Far East.

Will this be the end of the employment of raising the question of atomic, or now nuclear missiles in this context? Who knows.

Meanwhile, the Great Powers, and even some of the smaller powers, are vying for superiority in nuclear arms; and so the former are delicately and ditheringly poised on a knife's edge in fear of one another and are striving hard to this end to maintain their defence against a possible terrible holocaust, in which human and all natural life is at stake and will remain so for hundreds if not thousands of years before its effect passes off. If this state of preparedness or deteridness is the price of peace in our time so be it. Although so costly it has become a matter of 'Your money or your life!' 'Erring man is learning to handle Divine Fire'.

The Medical Authorities are well aware of the possible disastrous results and are making an effort to combat them. In such an eventuality Triage, which ignores moral or emotional issues (horrible thought) when casualties are many and resources few, will become the order of the day. This approach is irreplaceable when the sorter has to decide what dose of radiation each one has received and is likely to survive.

RAD, the unit of absorbed ionized radiation, varies from 50 to 150 RAD's to kill. All known precautions must be taken. What would have happened if Noah, seeing the approaching flood, had thrown up his hands saying 'this is a plumber's job'?

At this point the question of 'fall out' and atomic waste has to be considered the sources of which are, of course, the result of atomic explosions in tests (but, thank goodness, not so far in these parts), in the production of nuclear energy and the waste from them. No doubt more than due attention is being paid by our Scientists to this problem. It cannot be thrown away and dumped in anybody's back garden and be forgotten. It will remain, for hundreds of years, before it becomes inert. This is a big matter and, no doubt, our researchers will take advantage and eventually find a means of rendering it innocuous; but it would take a lot of time and expense — though perhaps it would provide a good deal of employment in associated trades. What become's of the fall out from the atomic explosion? Matter cannot be created or destroyed. I was told by a close relative of a celebrated scientist, who was staying in Ruthin some 13 or 14 years ago, that after being rocketed and shot into space, the resulting particles, coalesce and form a new planet eventually. This was not evidently in the mind of the Hymnist when he wrote '. . . Oh, may no earth-born cloud arise to hide Thee from Thy servant's eyes'.

In 1932 Sir James Chadwick split the atom, releasing from the proton, amongst others, its most important constituent, the Neutron, discovered in 1935, which has no electric charge, and has a selective action in penetrating certain tissues. This property led to the discovery of the Cyclotron — a device for accelerating the propulsion of neuclear rays at very high speeds. Thus it is possible to bombard certain areas of cancer inaccessible to surgery, without damage to the surrounding tissues.

Too little, I think, is known generally about this great man, James Chadwick, whose work will remain a landmark for many years to come. He came to reside in Denbigh for a few years, and many of us were proud to have had the pleasure and honour of meeting him socially. It was his fond hope that the neutron would be employed for peaceful purposes only. Unfortunately this hope was dashed to the ground by the neutron's incorporation for other warlike purposes. This saddened Sir James and must have been a great disappointment to him.

Health

Looking back at history, mankind has undergone the hazards and rigours of the Ice Age and Stone Age together with other natural upheavals and holocausts such as earthquakes, famine, pestilence, to mention but a few; and we should consider ourselves lucky to be alive.

A few centuries ago there were two visitations of the Black Death (Bubonic Plague). This scourge lasted from the fourteenth to the seventeenth century, killing hundreds of thousands of people; until the tide was stemmed by the Great Fire of London in 1666.

Ruthin was not exempt from this scourge, which exacted a very heavy toll of life – communities disappeared completely leaving no trace of their former existence. It is probable that the Parish of Dog (Dogfeiling), was one of them.

But things have improved tremendously since those days, and since this is not a treatise of medicine, which would take a team of experts to compile, we will consider only a few which come to mind.

Smallpox: This was a killer, and there are many today, including doctors, who have never had any experience of the disease.

Scarlet Fever: A very highly infectious disease caused many deaths, but has now almost disappeared, since the introduction of antibiotics. Some of us have memories of wearing gowns wrung out in carbolic, likewise sheets similarly treated hung over the door of the sick room — to prevent the spread of infection — but more likely, I think, used as a psychological measure.

Tuberculosis: So rampant until a few years ago, has been eradicated to a very great extent, or at least controlled by surgery, antibiotics and other methods. The cure of T.B. in those days was thought by many to be forlorn hope, by assiduity and hard work on the part of workers in this field, most of these difficulties were overcome. New hospitals were built for the purpose all over the country, including 'King Edward VII Hospital for the Cure of Consumption' at Llangwyfan, all of which contributed to this achievement.

Diabetes: A debilitating disease, eventually causing the early death of the sufferer, was conquered by Insulin, prolonging life, and enabling those afflicted to lead a normal existence.

Diptheria: There are many today, including doctors, who have had no experience of this dread killing disease since the introduction of antibiotics, and it has become a rarity. In the old days it was very devastating, occurring very frequently and called for frantic effort on the part of doctors in combating it, which in many cases called for drastic surgical operation, including tracheotomy, to ensure the free entrance of air into the lungs.

The author knows of a case in which the diphtheritic membrane was so large and thick (teeming with bacteria) that the doctor grasped it with a pair of forceps and threw it into the open fire where, of course, it was destroyed. The patient in a few days made a full recovery and lived to become a singer of some repute.

Cancer: There are very few homes, where a visitation of this has not affected one member of the family or another, but nowadays it does not hold the dread to the same extent which it had a few years ago. Great efforts have, and are, being made for its eradication, and although a cure is not 'just around the corner', remarkable strides have and are being made by our researchers, with the implementation of highly sophisticated weaponry to bring about, if not a cure, cancer under control. As was the case in Tuberculosis, the cure of which was thought by many to be a forlorn hope, the assiduity and hard work of those of the Cancer Campaign has already brought cancer, to some extent, under control, and the effort is progressing daily.

It may, however, be little consolation to the sufferers and their families, to realise that there are worse diseases than cancer.

Some of the above diseases may, more or less, in their toll of ill health, be relegated to the part; with these diseases and many others (no less eminent and too numerous to mention) must be associated the names of Jenner (smallpox), Ronald Ross (for the discovery of the malarial parasite – Plasmodium Vivax), Banting (for his work and discovery of Insulin) and others.

The discoverers of antibiotics after the Second World War must not be forgotten; some of these have been the sheet anchor in the treatment of infectious and other diseases, such as Polio-myelitis (wrongly, for many years, termed Infantile Paralysis), Asthma, Tetanus, Whooping Cough, outstanding amongst which is Penicillin (Alexander Fleming).

The National Health Insurance has been a great factor in bringing the State Medical Science and Technological Service up to a very high standard. But, due credit and recognition must be given to the practitioners and scientists who, over the ages, have not by any 'hit or miss' methods laid down the foundations, on which modern medicine in this country, is built. All this has been accomplished without many of the available present day resources.

The National Health Service

The fertile conception of the Beveridge Plan in which the suffering humanity was to be cared for by fit and able bodied who were in full employment. This wonderful idea was carried into effect by the then brilliant Health Minister, Aneurin Bevan, in 1948. He promised the country a free Health Service for all, and this was, and is, a boon to everyone in this country and, with its excellence, an envy to most of the civilized West. Why, people from abroad come for treatment, including surgical operations, confinements and so on. This went on for some years but changing world conditions, including monetary values, has caused some modification in this respect. With all the goodwill in the World, you cannot legislate for happiness for all. Nevertheless, it is our great mainstay and hope for the future of the health of the country.

Medical and scientific advances have progressed so rapidly that during the past fifty or sixty years, more has been learnt and discovered than from the beginning of time, with the result that a sixth form boy studying biology can know more about them than his celebrated ancestors.

It cannot be denied that until the early 20th century poverty existed in most parts of the country. The author remembers in the early 1920's an old man (age 66 or 67) holding up his fist saying 'Thank God for Lloyd George and the old age pension' (of 10s a week or was it 5s?).

As children, most of us were in receipt of our Saturday penny, which was looked forward to eagerly, notwithstanding the fact that we had all the moderate luxuries called for. On one Saturday, I went to the grocer's, which supplied a 1d bar of chocolate, each of goodly amount, when a boy came in and asked for a pennoth of bacon fat which was supplied by an assistant, who told me after the boy had gone 'that will be the boy's dinner'.

The days of children going about in bare feet and ragged clothes are long since passed and, since the introduction of the Welfare State, and even for some time before that, there was no excuse for rank poverty, except among those who were unable to claim, for one reason or another the helpful benefits offered and available, and to which they were entitled.

Nowadays, one might hear a *pater familias* say to his small child who was bent on having a bicycle, or some such thing, 'In my days we could not afford to have bicycles', to which would come the ready rejoinder 'Aren't you glad you live with us now Dad?'

Man has marvelled at the Universe and wondered what indeed is the Nature of Life and what is it's purpose — are we living in a dream or what? The secret has been probed since the beginning of time and this has meant intricate caluculations involving figures of regarding millions and even trillions in time and space which are quite incomprehensible to the lay mind, and theories have been evolved to endeavour to assess their accuracy. We have Darwin's 'the origin of species', Enstein's theory of relativity, Plato's Quantum theory and, more recently, the Big Bang, all of which still leaves us in great uncertainty. When did it occur? From whence came the essentials for its production? We must remain perplexed and bewildered and at present content ourselves with imagining that they were at a time and place called Infinity and probably will remain so for all time.

Health is the greatest treasured gift we have and, in many cases, perhaps the least appreciated until we are struck down by illness or ageing when, for even metals tire, we would think or exclaim, 'I wish to God that I were fit and strong and active again'. Money will not buy back good health and so we should all follow what many of us interpret to be the tenets contained in the original Beveridge Report. Who would have imagined the immensity which the perplexity of the New Health Service project was assumed, and no doubt will assume, with its consequent intrusions into the interstices of ordinary every day life. Putting aside the organization as a whole we, the general public, can only consider some of its individual aspects, one by one, As a General Practitioner (Retired) one is astounded by the terrific cost alone of many items, in the armoury of highly, to mention but a few, technical, sophisticated weapons such as X-rays, Scanners, Cyclotron, to combat disease; there are other departments to be catered for, and there is no bottomless 'money box', to provide for all the needs, necessities and maintenance of all these services.

We have been slow in evaluating the importance of the physical (sexual) and intellectual faculties in our individual lives; for no doubt the former reproduction is predominant, from which the latter emanates.

Our education, starting from the '3 R's' (Reading, wRiting and aRithmetic) has brought us up to a very high standard of intellectuality but, in too many cases, has not made us amenable to the '3 C's' (Cool, Calm and Collected), meaning to control, which must be derived from environmental sources. This is not to say that we are the subjects of Predestination, but our fate is governed by the exercise of both, in various degrees, in parading our thoughts and actions to proper perspective.

It is pleasing to see that education authorities and others are recognising this and the permissive age, in spite of its other faults, viz. disruption of family life in many instances, is showing us how to gain, to some extent, health and satisfaction in the sexual extent. Specialist well-trained personnel should be available in schools and clinics to instruct children and young adults in their behaviour in sexual problems. This, no doubt, would assist to alleviate the frustration of supression and other feelings giving rise to neuroses and other undesirable conditions.

The advice on contraception, whether to limit the population or for other reasons, must rest with the Medical Profession, and not with the layman, as they are unqualified to give an opinion on such questions as test tube babies, artificial insemination and other methods.

At maturity, with our inherent desire for love mongering, the sex urge is predominant and no woman who wants to exercise the right to have a baby should be denied this natural urge.

This is not to say that everyone is subject to predestination, and the question arises 'Are the effects in our make-up of any aberrations genetic or environmental and so amenable to control? We are sufficiently educated, but not yet fully amenable to control.

D.N.A. (Deoxyribonucleic Acid)

For some years we have known the structure and arrangement of the molecules which go to make the living protoplasm, however it was 'triggered off' to action and, except for those destined to proceed further in biology, we left it at that.

Since then, and particularly during the last few years, very specialised researches by Crick and Watson and others have discovered the wonderful molecule and fundamental material of heredity — D.N.A. From this the chromosomes are derived (23 pairs in each), and from these, after being denuded of most of their protein, are able to carry messages and direction of heredity, from cell to cell, finally to the various vital areas of the body. Why should we go into such detail, in this article about this wonderful discovery? It is because all of us non-sientific people are implicated, and many of us may individually be forced to make a decision involving spiritual, religious, moral, emotional or mental scruples, relating to heredity, as we shall see later. So much has appeared in the media, and broadcast on the television, which make some of us hesitate to come to a conclusion or, more likely a confusion.

Amniocentesis: This is the withdrawal of amniotic fluid containing foetal cells, through the maternal abdominal wall, by a hollow needle. The chromesomes of the cells are examined and, by this means, it is possible to determine with some degree of certainty the sex of the unborn child and whether or not it is likely to develop a mental or physical defect. This so far has not been extended and I hope it never will be to criminality, i.e. to estimation of predestined criminal tendencies. What action, if any, is to be taken in the matter? It is advisable that the best advice should be sought in an effort to control tendencies of all kinds. Nevertheless, the decision is left *ad finem* to the unfortunate parents.

In this context the two following episodes fairly typify, I think, some of the human and moral issues. Let researchers proceed, but with caution, allowing free choice to remain, without attempting to change the character, by addition or subtraction of the individual.

Case 1: Mrs. X suffered from Pernicious Anaemia for a few years during which time she aborted on 3 or 4 occasions, the last being 1930, which produced twin foetuses at 4-$4\frac{1}{2}$ months. The Pernicious Anaemia was treated by the only known remedies at the time, i.e. liver extracts and iron.

Then in 1930 whole blood transfusion was employed, the husband being the donor at the local Cottage Hospital. This was simplified by the fact that the Rhesus Factor was not at this time recognised generally. She progressed, it appeared, successfully until 1931, when she again became pregnant; and near full term it was decided that she should be delivered by Caesarean Section at the local hospital — to try and avoid unnecessary strain, haemorrhage, etc. An eminent Obstetrician was employed for the purpose, and at the time of delivery it was decided, by he Obstetrician, and the author himself, that if the child appeared norman in every respect the parturient should be sterilized and this appeared to be the case.

Some weeks after the birth the child began to develop some of the stigmata indicating what is now called the Down's Syndrome. In spite of this the parents were delighted with their offspring and lavished great kindness, love, gentleness and encouragement on the child. The mother died two or three years after the boy's birth, but he still was very well cared for by his stepmother who later had married his father.

This care and devotion brought forth, in spite of his obvious defect, a liking for good music — from gramophone records, and an uncanny knowledge of the football teams engaged in the 'Pools'. This happy state continued for 41 years, until his death as a result of an accident playing football.

Case 2: On the night of 31st December 1931, I was called to attend a confinement at a cottage. The bedroom was small and lit by a small oil lamp, precluding the use of ether anaesthetic. However, I usually carried with me on these occasions a Boyle's Gas and Oxygen apparatus.. The District Nurse was in attendance. Labour proceeded normally and the patient gave birth to a female child. On examining the latter it was found that she was suffering from a meningo myelocoele. What was to be done under the circumstances? Anyhow, the exposed part was cleaned as well as possible with a weak antiseptic, the sciatic plexus reposed gently with a pair of forceps, into as satisfactory niche as possible in the vertebral canal and the whole stitched in three layers; theca, serous and vascular layer and finally the dermic area, with fine catgut, thus the wound was closed — it healed satisfactorily by first intention.

There was no resulting infection of the wound; but of course there was paraplegia and some slight degree of hydocephalus, which became accentuated as time went on. In spite of all this, the child lived to almost three years of age, with loving care and attention from her mother and from the four other children of the family.

The above appeared to be the solution of some such cases at the time with not altogether unhappy results.

With the advances in neurological and microsurgery and the ready availability to a specialised hospital no doubt the above would have been treated differently at the present time.

The Permissive Age

We have been wafted into the permissive age and our ideas of the mode of life have changed considerably and how such problems involving emotional, moral, religious (putting aside the economical) scruples and allowing full play for plausibility are to be dealt with. *Ad finem* this overwhelmingly difficult and serious decision rests with parents who may rue or view the consequences with serene satisfaction or not. It is not for any of of us to moralize on this issue.

We are living in the permissive age, how different it seems to many of us older people! We were expected to conform to the high standards of moral behaviour exhorted by our elders. The whole idea of sex was pooh-poohed or brushed aside as if it did not exist, at any rate, many parents 'were not amused'. In spite of this not much harm seems to have resulted, except perhaps to arouse retrospectively some resentment (or even jealousy) in the so-called freedom many of the younger people enjoy now.

Many homes during the earlier nursery period were familiar with naughty rude jargon such as:

> Pee, po piddle
> Belly, bum, drawers

and the little girls, not to be outdone, would add 'District Nurse!' and so on. Scratch the veneer of this exemplary upbringing and we would release a torrent of words and phrases, in many cases some of which the ordinary person had never heard.

From here we go on to school age, when boys and girls were encouraged to associate with those of the opposite sex, by going to dances, concerts and entertainments together — in which there was kissing, cuddling, following amusing conversation, the

71

boy seeing his partner home, but it would end here. Of course, this natural pursuit of lovemongering will persist for all time.

Passing out of parental control to a large extent these young people are left to their own devices, to learn the things of life, sometimes in the wrong way. It is surprising how much the young people do know. Both father and mother are away from home most of the time, in many cases, and are unable through timidity, ignorance, hypocrisy or guilty conscience, to offer sound advice when asked how their libido was gratified; the father, 'H'm ah, yes . . . . You'll have to think it out for yourself', or more likely, in the cowardly way, 'Ask your mother', who then, when asked, would be similarly perplexed except to adjure the young person to 'be good'. This is out of keeping, in these days, it would probably be 'be careful', which advice perhaps may result in a frustrating neurosis guilt complex and the like; some of whom may pay pennance for the things they haven't done; in finding outlets for their emotions.

Maturity in both sexes appears to have arrived at a much earlier age than formerly and, with it, the age of consent is reduced to 14 years, in some cases. With rape, due to various contingencies such as fear, threats of violence, etc., the law does not fully accept 'consent' as a defence until the exercise of the will is made after the act.

This question along with that of contraception places us in a quandry and it is doubtful if anyone is able to pronounce judgement in any particular area.

And in this issue later, we have no right to moralize or criticise in other peoples 'private lives', human nature being what it is, how many of our own would stand up to investigations? I think that most of us, at one time or another, have thought or imagined ourselves performing extravagent or even outrageous acts of which we should be ashamed in retrospect but have not had the guts to carry them out, perhaps we are little better than those who do!

Not only have they matured earlier, but successive generations from the olden times have shown the trend to become increased in stature. We pictured the knights of old as being huge men in their shining armour; on measuring their casements, it will be

72

found that they were designed for much smaller men than those of the present generation. Whether these will be as tough as in their parents time alone will show. It is obvious that children grow up nowadays to be bigger than their parents, the builders of the future will have to look out for they will have to 'raise the roof' or at any rate the lintel over the doorways.

Before leaving parental control we must consider the question of vaccination or inoculation against threat of an impending disease which may cause an adverse iatrogenic effect upon the child, or even death. This is so at present in the case of whooping cough especially and where there is any doubt about the advisability of this procedure, parents should consult their doctor to assess any tendency or allergy of these effects and any suspected contra-indication for vaccination.

Spare Part Surgery

By this is meant the replacement of a malfunctioning organ by transplant of a healthy one; it is not as easy as it seems to be, for the material available from the donor must be compatible in every respect of that of the intended recipient. Moreover, the criteria laid dow, including ethical, moral and other issues, have to be taken into consideration, as well as those of the donor's relatives (or guardians) and the latter have the last word in the matter. There has been great controversy among the public in general lately, in determining life or death of an individual donor.

There are two kinds of death, viz :

1. Molecular death, that is death of all the individual cells in the body. This is manifest by post mortem cooling and was, until recently, the only and absolute criterion.

2. Somatic death of the organism as a whole. The medical profession have gone to infinite and exhaustive research, employing all the clinical acumen of eminent authorities with the help of complex mechanical means to elucidate this cause of death. So we may rest assured that the individual is beyond all methods of resuscitation, and any action taken.

73

Lastly, there is the freedom of relatives and others to exercise of the Will in these cases. Of course, so much has been written and televised although much of it incomprehensible to the public, they may express their feelings freely. Nevertheless there is a crying need at the present time for kidney transplant material and appeal for that must, and probably will, soon be heeded.

Ruthin Hospital

The Board of Guardians built an addition, away from the Workhouse, which was completed in 1915, in the form of a Workhouse Infirmary. This served its purpose for a short time in that capacity, serving the County; when it was realized that the accommodation and facilities were in excess of the Institution's requirements and that greater and better use could be made of them. After negotiation with the Welsh Board of Health with a request that the Hospital should be opened for all the patients of all the doctors in the area, a very unusual and unprecedented arrangement, and that Body graciously sanctioned the project. We have to thank their Chief Medical Officer, the late Dr. Llewelyn Williams, for his help in bringing this into effect.

It was a boon to patients and doctors alike, although it placed an added heavy responsibility and the exercising of a great deal of tact on the part of the Medical Officer (Dr. J. Medwyn Hughes), the Superintendent (Mr. Humphrey Morris) and the Hospital Staff. In spite of this most of the inherent difficulties were overcome satisfactorily, and so the facilities were invaluable to the residents of Ruthin and district. It became a very busy and indispensable hospital calling, when required, the assistance of the Physicians and Surgeons of Ruthin Castle Clinic, Liverpool, Chester and Wrexham and of course Mr. H. Morriston Davies, who came to live in this area in the early 1920's, and was a tower of strength in its furtherance.

We must not forget the efforts of men like Rowland Jones, Meurig Roberts, Bob Mostyn and others also, for their efforts in organizing the 'Fund' in aid, and the 'Penny in the Pound' scheme locally which helped the more needy to cover their hospital expenses.

The Hospital has undergone great structural alterations recently, and is now a First Class Hospital for the admission of various diseases not requiring operation.

In the Air

The crowning glory of this year (1982) as far as progress is concerned, is the launching into space of the American shuttle *Columbia,* with its two astronauts, which filled the whole world with amazement, for it was blasted into space to fulfil a mission to travel many thousands of miles at a speed of thousands of M.P.H., encircling the earth thirty-six times, and returning to a narrow runway, on time, or at least only a few seconds late. This was a wonderful example of skill and endurance on the part of the astronauts and the skill and know-how of the builders of the craft. For the men had to be specially trained in technology and to endure all the hazards called upon them, and last, but not least, the designers who had produced a heat shield capable of resisting over 2,000 degrees Fahrenheit, all of which ensured a safe landing after its passage through the stratosphere. Surely this is the beginning of a shuttle service in air and space travel if indeed it has not already occurred in 1983.

It has always been the ambition of many to run faster, to climb higher, or dive deeper, etc., etc., than our fellow men. One is reminded of children, at an early age, playing a game of bending over the side of a bridge and seeing who could bend the furthest — well eventually someone suceeds, often toppling into the water in the river below. This does not always happen though and the competitive drive is still there and will, no doubt, continue for all time.

If you asked the average small boy forty years ago, from whatever stratum of life, what he was going to be when he grew up, the answer would invariably be 'I am going to be an engine driver' meaning the driver of a 'puffer train'. Today it would be a space man. The ambition to be an engine driver remained for many years, during which time nursery floors, kitchen floors or wherever there was space, were littred with yards and yards of toy railway lines. Even in some schools, space was set aside to encourage the young idea to become 'railway minded'. Later on, the motor trade came into being, and boys fell for the idea of driving one. It is amazing how young farm hands became adept in driving, and what is more, reversing with an articulated vehicle in tow — a real work of art.

Then came the electrification of the railway. In spite of his excellent plans and ideas, Beeching did what he was asked to do, but was, in the opinion of many, wrongly briefed. Electrification for North Wales came no further than Crewe, and with that omission has left us marooned as far as the railway system is concerned, and surely this must be rectified.

Notwithstanding all this, we older people in these parts remember the thrilling exploits of Bleriot in his monoplane flying over the English Channel, or Grahame White in his biplane and we have always kept pace with the idea of air travel as a means for business or pleasure purposes.

Who will forget the daring exploits and achievements of that intrepid airman, Vivian Vaughan Davies Hewitt, born in 1888 who came to live at 'The Warren', Bodfari, until he was eleven years old, during which time he spoke Welsh. We can remember seeing him coasting down the Welsh coastline on a summer evening to Llandudno, where his headquarters lay at that time, during his earlier attempts to attain a mastery in aviation. His efforts were crowned with success and culminated in his epic solo flight across the Irish Sea on 26th April 1912, from Rhyl to Phoenix Park, Dublin. This made him the first man to accomplish this feat — a distance of 75 miles — and so he became world famous.

After the second World War, the novelty of flying, or at any rate of going up into the air, caught on rapidly with many.

I remember visiting a Travelling Air Circus, outside Ruthin, where one was taken for a trip around the vicinity — it was in the days when one had to hold one's hat on whilst flying — and on looking down over the fuselage, such was one's feeling of exultation and superiority, as our fellow men in the street appeared as ground lice!

A friend of mine, Lloyd Mainwaring learnt to fly at Brooklands and his first aeroplane, an Avro, cost £110. 'Very third hand' as he said, being bought from the Slough War Trading Estate. After putting up a hangar at his home in Dolbelidr, Trefnant, he acquired and disposed of (at four different times) five planes, the last one being registered with the letters G-A. DFC, the same as the old 'much cherished' Denbighshire motor registration. He and a friend crossed the Channel fourteen or was it 20 times between 1930 and 1938, visiting five or six different countries.

Since then several prototypes of areoplanes have come into existence some of which fly at thousands of miles per hour, notably the Concorde, the most magnificent supersonic aeroplane ever built. Although all planes are pressurised for various heights encountered, the question of differences in local times, as between ourselves and the various countries to be visited, will have to be considered individually for the purpose of sleep and rest — thus for instance a 2 a.m. departure from this country will mean 9 p.m. yesterday arrival in New York, or 6 p.m. in Los Angeles, so we will have to attune ourselves to these variations. Shades of Jules Vernes 'Round the World in 80 days', his fascinating fictional novel, shows how twenty four hours could have been lost in that period in this way.

No doubt these difficulties will be accentuated and overcome now that we have appeared to begin the space age for all.

It is not generally known that a place for a landplane terminal between UK and Canada, or raher for transatlantic passenger flights on the West Coast, was being considered in the late 1930's. Amongst these considerations were, the suitability of the site regarding air conditions, i.e. fog, the winds, large flat area of land (which is what a radar station likes for the propogation of radio waves) and the making of runways, free from obstruction to ingress and exit and, most important of all, the turbulent international situation at the time, when war clouds were gathering. The area between Abergele, Bodelwyddan, Rhuddlan and Towyn fulfilled all the natural desiderata, particularly with regard to being comparatively fog free and, in this respect, 'Sunny Rhyl' was not a misnomer.

After what one would imagine to have been massive deliberation, Prestwick was chosen as an Airport. What a boost this could have been to the Vale of Clwyd, making it an important international airport, with all its associated requirements.

The project can only be regarded as a 'near miss'. 'What a blessing that we never miss the things we never had', had the project succeeded! The natural characteristics remain, the mountains, the flat terrain, air conditions and the prevailing equable weather, still remain for all time and for the provisional requirements of future generations — who knows?!

Before bailing out from the air, mention must be made of some of the episodes during the last war, for instance the crashing of a bomber plane at Llanfair, carrying thirteen members of a headquarters staff of the RAF in its fllight from a base in Ireland to another destination in which, in the space of a few minutes, an idyllic summer afternoon was transformed into one of carnage, in which the whole complement perished, as the aircraft burst into flames in the air.

Also at Bryn Eglwys a bomber from one of the night flying stations got into trouble and a fire seemed to have occured. The Commander ordered the crew to 'bale out' which they did, parachuting onto the various objects on the ground. The rear gunner who found difficulty in ejecting himself from the plane, was the last to leave and he landed on the corrugated iron roof of a large barn, making the last part of his interrupted descent the most perilous of all. Happily, the pilot managed to skilfully land the plane at its air station safely with no loss of life.

There were two or three incidents in the district in which the pilots of practising fighter planes baled out with not such happy consequences.

From the beginning of the war we were all very much ARP minded — every man, woman and child had been provided with a gas mask and one enthusiastic dear old lady went so far as to consider the question of having an air raid shelter in her garden. Whether this was erected, I just forget, but who could have thought of her house on the outskirts of Ruthin as being a likely target for a bombing attack. Anyhow, the bombers came to Liverpool and delivered their most devastating attack on that city, during which an ammunition ship was said to have been blown up and, being attacked and pursued by our fighters, the bombers, to lighten their load and help their escape, jettisoned their bombs indiscriminately. A stick of three or four bombs was dropped between Rhewl and the outskirts of Ruthin — one landing in a field a few hundred yards from the old lady's house. After the major bombing attack on Liverpool and district exploding, and causing a great deal of noise but no apparent damage, our old lady slept peacefully through the night, but the next night was tortured by the sound of some thunder which was in the air.

Field Sports and Pastimes

Snowdon and Cader Idris have been, and still are, splendid areas for the pursuit of mountaineering, that hazardous and often perilous activity.

What is the call which urges these enthusiasts to get to the top of a high mountain or rock? The only answer I have heard of is 'Because it is there!' This indominatable urge is typified by the wonderful achievement in the conquest of Mount Everest by an expedition to the Himalayas, sponsored by the Royal Geographical Society and the Alpine Club, and led by John Hunt, in May 1953, which party included amongst other famous men, Robert Cecil Evans, who played a vital part in the conquest of Everest. Where is the word 'cwm' in relation to the Western Head derived from, surely it is from the Welsh 'cwm' meaning valley. However, we must claim that he is one of us, his grandparents (W. R. Evans, late clerk of the Peace and Clerk to the Denbighshire County Council), lived for many years in Ruthin, as did his parents. Sir Robert Cecil Evans is, and has been for some years, Principal of the University College of North Wales at Bangor.

Another mountaineer of note was that intrepid climber Eric Roberts of Ruthin, who, on an American Expedition Annapurna, in September 1979, lost his life by the fall of an avalanche.

Fox Hunting

Hunting and fishing for food have, from the earliest times, been the pre-occupation of man. We have read about that big chap St. Peter and others fishing in the Sea of Galilee.

There seems to have been hunting of the deer on horseback in these parts of the Vale of Clwyd during the past 150 years but not foxhunting. Richard Heaton of the Hunt and Simon Lloyd, son of Colonel Rod Lloyd who was Master, both say that there is no record of the Hunt meeting in Ruthin district and that Moel Famau was probably as far as they went. The hounds were at one time kept at Mostyn and Pengwern before Cefn and some were at Coed Coch and the hounds could not have walked as far as Ruthin for the meet.

It is only in fairly recent motorized days when roads got so busy that hounds may have been taken to a meet (R.H. said that). In Ruthin area the local farmers etc., had to deal with foxes themselves by getting together any kind of pack of dogs and having a shoot. This was called a 'bobbery'.

As the hunt was mainly down the Denbigh end of the Vale, Sir Ernest Tate built stabling etc., for his horses at Trefnant, because of the distance from Pool Park, which was his residence. He later came to live in Galltfaenan for some years and the stable premises in Trefnant were converted into a fine house, with a very large and delightful garden.

Cock Fighting

Was a very popular pastime in the 18th century. The breed employed was the game fowl, and the venue was in the Llanfair District, where in Bryn Chwarae may be seen a number of hollows, which were unmistakeably old cock-pits.

There was a cock-pit at the rear of the White Lion, Ruthin, now the Castle Hotel, which has disappeared. The fine Stuart cock-pit, which was once located at the rear of the Hawk and Buckle in Denbigh, is now to be seen at St. Fagan's Welsh Folk Museum, Cardiff. An example of a fine ancient building on a modern alien site!

Cock fighting came to an end in 1849 following an Act of Parliament levying very servere penalties for its non-observance.

Bull Baiting

This cruel sport of tying a bull to a post to be baited by dogs was a very popular form of entertainment on the Market Square (St. Peter's Square) in Ruthin during the 18th century. The bull chain for the baiting was held by the Warden and Church-wardens of St. Peter's. Any person wishing to bait bulls had to pay one shilling to the Church authorities for the hire of the chain and return it in good condition after the bait. There are many entries in the Churchwardens' Accounts recording repairs to the bull chain.

The sport remained popular until it was prohibited, by Act of Parliament in 1835.

Rabbit Coursing

I remember attending this (so called) sport when a boy on two different occasions (it would be about 1909 or 1910); they were well patronized. It would have ended very soon after these years. People have an aversion to cruelty. Again, as a boy, I and two or three friends would visit a nearby slaughterhouse to assist in pulling the rope to point the animals head down as the butcher wielded his brutal old fashioned pole-axe (now merci-fully replaced by much more humanitarian methods) shouting 'give him another one Johnnie'; the callous little wretches! On being reproved by our parents such ideas became everlasting abhorrent immediately.

We must take a broad minded and realist view of food, according to our feelings, emotions, taste or necessity. Quite a number of people enjoy pheasant, cold partridge (when you can get it), chicken (or even in its neotonus form, the egg), or roast lamb, notwithstanding the idea that even farmers may come under the doubtful category of wrong doers by some.

Outdoor Sports and Pastimes

Football-Soccer (Association Football) was the only football played in Ruthin and district until Ruthin School went over to Rugby. Although we are a small area, Ruthin Football Club from about 1874 onwards, produced five international players. They were, John Roberts, the two Owen brothers, Jack Humphreys and Uriah Goodwin. There were others just as good, Price Mostyn, who lived to be 101 and six months, Jack and his brother Dai Thomas, and others too numerous to mention.

Rugby — After Football came Rugby and in a very short time Ruthin raised a Club of a very high standard whose team is the equal of many in North Wales and the neighbouring Counties. Ruthin School produced an International Rugby Player; a very rare occasion for a North Wallian! He was M. G. Roberts from Colwyn Bay, who in 1960 was capped for Wales and toured New Zealand with the British Lions in 1971.

In February 1984, the Ruthin Rugby Club hosted, for the first time, a youth team from the South of France.

Hockey — In 1919 we formed a mixed Hockey Club, and it went ahead during the first two seasons to produce four Welsh International Hockey Players, viz Glyn Jones, David Jones (Dai John), H. M. Roberts and P. D. Jones. The terrain around Ruthin has always lent itself for all kinds of outdoor sports and pastimes, such as cricket, golf, croquet and so on.

Cricket — This sport used to be considered almost as a way of life at school and many of us have spent hours, after changing into cricket flannels, watching two of the team perfom at the wicket, while nine of the other twenty two players sat on a bench with the more patient of us shouting 'good shot, Sir' or 'well bowled', while some of the more impatient of us were saying beneath our breath. 'get to hell out of it and let me have my innings!' which when our turn came would often result in 'out first ball'.

Even so, cricket has, to a very great extent, in spite of certain rowdiness in recent years, retained its high impeccable standard as a well conducted game. Most sports and pastimes have now become organized and commercialized, with all its benefits, also its detractions.

R. A. Lloyd, a teacher at Ruthin School, was a prominent in this area. Up to about the 1920's there were two cricket teams in this district. The Ruthin Cricket Club and one at Llanychan; the former included Albert Thomas, who later became Northampton's fast bowler; Arthur Tyldesley (cousin of the great Lancashire player of that name), George Higginson, Goronwy Williams and Goronwy Rowlands (near relative of H. M. Stanley).

The other team consisted, amongst others, of C. C. Mott (who with his wife wrote some excellent novels amongst which were *Sting of the Whip*, *A Gentleman of No Family* and others), Frodsham Lund, Dr. Grace Calvert, R. O. Jones, Robert Blackley, Captain Hawke and Dr. J. W. Anderson.

One of the best cricketers produced by Ruthin School was Robert (Bob) Barber, who was a Cambridge Blue for Cricket and Athletics. During the 1950's he captained Lancashire and Warwickshire Cricket Clubs; and played in twenty-eight Tests for England.

Other Sports

Of course tennis, bowls, lacrosse, swimming and badminton have, for some years, been enjoyed and, in recent years, swimming in the baths provided by the D.C.C. (now Clwyd Brynhyfryd School.

Facilities for ice skating have not been provided, but no doubt this enjoyable exercise will soon be provided for.

We must not lose our identity, our language, or any of our culture. Many people in their youth have gone away from Wales to seek a livelihood abroad and, after many years and perhaps success, have had a *Hiraith* (longing or yearning) to return to their native heath, with is charm in the language, its music and homeliness and its homing instinct, often typified in its hymns and songs. Many of the hymns and songs are characterized by their homing instinct in their metre.

The Language

The language, if not regarded as an ancient classical one, is an ancient one retaining certain accents (the circumflex for example) its mutations and slurs, and the two latter making them almost imperceptibly for translation to music. Again Welsh has its genders to qualify many of its nouns, such as *dau* (m) or *dwy* (f). The misappropriation in some cases can give rise to quite a different meaning to the intended one. It is also an easy vehicle for poetry, especially lyric poetry. The language is much more popular than some non-Welsh people may think. It has been taught in most schools in Wales and immigrant children have picked it up readily, much to the embarrassment of their parents — the latter in its usage by its children are fast falling into the habit of speaking Welsh.

Music

Ruthin can boast a number of musicians, in the way of conductors and individual performers — W. A. Lloyd (Ruthin Choral Society) with productions of *Messiah* (Handel), *Rose Maiden* (Cowan) *Stabat Mater* (Dvorak) and others, R. Harris Jones, in great demand at *Cymanfaoedd Canu* and *Eisteddfodau*, winning the mixed choir competition at the National Eisteddfod in 1912, W. G. Hodgson who, with his local production of a series of Gilbert and Sullivan Light Operas and last, but not least, in the forties the Ruthin Choral Society, formed by Mrs. Violet Evans of Ardwyn and under the superb coaching and conductorship of Morgan Nicholas (who succeeded Sir Walford Davies as Director of Music for Wales) performed works which included Handel's *Messiah,* Haydn's *Creation, Stabat Mater* (Dvorak), *Hiawatha* and Brahms's *Requiem.*

A few individuals made their mark at Covent Garden, Glynbourne and in opera in many towns in this country and abroad. They were, to mention but two, Furness Williams and Charles Moorhouse. But the outstanding one in opera who made a meteoric rise in fame to become a soprano of world-wide repute, was Joan Carlisle.

There were others who made their mark as soloists in

Cathedral Festivals, in Recitals at the Wigmore and Aeolian Halls and at various oratorio concerts in this country and in London such as Muriel Hughes. One must not fail to mention Johnnie Williams, a natural singer, who delighted audiences in Ruthin and the surrounding district for many years and, one year, won the Blue Ribbon at the National Eisteddfod for his effort.

It is delightful to know that in Ruthin there is in existence an amateur operatic company, who perform Gilbert and Sullivan and other works periodically. Lastly, the Ruthin Music Club — founded in 1945 and still flourishing, have engaged over the years some famous artistes to perform, such as, Carl Dolmetsch, Jack Brymer, Osian Ellis, Julian Lloyd Webber, Rohan Sarman, Alan Schiller, Yaltah Menuhin, Isobel Baillie, Gwyneth Jones and Norma Procter.

Epilogue

In spite of far reaching research the mystery of how the universe came into being has not been disclosed; man has always had an unsatiable urge to delve into the 'unknown' from times of old.

'They that go down to the sea in ships and occupy their their business in great waters. These men see the works of the Lord and his wonders in the deep'. (Psalm CVII : 23, 24).

Human beings during recent years have made diapedetic* intrusions into space with this in mind. How much knowledge they have gained it is too early to estimate, but they have not returned 'empty handed' by any means. In this vast 'space', outside our own orbit, which extends to infinity, they have experienced an environment far different from ours, for instance 'weightlessness' (walking in space), telepathy and, possibly, empathy. Some of these have been experienced by those who have flown to great heights in our own sphere. For instance, the young air pilot in the Second World War, who got into trouble with his plane high up in the sky and panicked, regained normal composure by the 'presence' of his mother (deceased) and was directed back to earth safely.

One, at least, of those who had put a foot on the moon was so affected that he was aware of a 'presence', and was convinced of this.

Now these perceptions or impressions cannot be too lightly dismissed as hallucinations or just imagination. Thus the human aura as may be thought by many people, which cannot be perceived normally, except to a few with artificial aid, is known to exist and is inseparable from the outer world. Is this the reason

---

* Term used for migration of blood corpuscles through the confines of the blood vessels.

in the early Christian days saints and other holy men were depicted with a halo over the uncovered parts of the body?

Perception, i.e. to be aware through the five senses, is not given in the same degree to everybody. There are lights and colours beyond the solar spectrum, which may be observed by some under exceptionally favourable circumstances. Again, certain sounds remain outside the human auditory range, what is music to us may be discord or cacophony to dogs and they register their disapproval by howling, as if in pain. Some creatures have not the same sense of eyesight as we know it, such as bats and, I suppose, moles, who are not without eyes if only rudimentary (no, Nature has not forgotten to 'dot' the i's)! and dolphins who have them but exist for a great part of their lives in muddy water — and they employ echo location or sonar. This method which we copied and used to great effect in World War II was the basis on which **RADAR** was founded.

Therefore, our awareness is not to be ignored, as it may touch, although remotely and imperfectly, on the fringe of the mystery of a divinity. With this thought and having considered many other things of which we know practically nothing, we must press on hopefully day by day in our daily toil. Then, at the close of the day, after the irksome tasks and chores are over, the dust after the struggle having settled down, the sweat and tears dried, and having shaken hands with our rivals — they were not too badly really! – relax, forget about holocausts, pulsars and leave all those kind of things to the scientists — they may never happen, at least not in our lifetime. We are foolish enough not to perceive that there is a greater force in existence than nuclear energy, but it may take ages to be brought fully into effect, and that is Love — without which the world would not exist — and in the end it will find a way.

So what of the future?

> Our fate is linked not solely with the stars that shine,
> But by the force of Love Divine,
> Providing mysteriously the means
> Of mingling and coupling our parental genes.

So what next? Well, your guess is as good as, and perhaps better than, mine.